The Political Economy of Change

The Political Economy of Change

*Papers presented to Section F (Economics)
at the 1974 Annual Meeting of the British
Association for the Advancement of Science*

Edited by K. J. W. Alexander

Basil Blackwell · Oxford · 1975

0 631 16540 1

Set in Linotype Times
Printed in Great Britain
by Western Printing Services Ltd., Bristol
and bound at The Pitman Press Ltd., Bath

Contents

Introduction

The interaction of economics and politics stimulated by the prospects of change was an obviously appropriate theme for discussion when the British Association's Annual Meeting was held in Scotland in September 1974. The papers now published, when read at Stirling to the Economics Section, provided the basis for such a discussion.

Taken together these papers present a view broader and more interdisciplinary than contemporary economists usually favour. The eighteenth century Scottish moralists and political economists would have been very much at home, intellectually as well as geographically, with even the most technical of the economics papers (Sadler) being concerned with general welfare.

The impact of economics on politics, and in particular of inflation on democracy and of disparities in regional prosperity, coupled with North Sea oil on the concord of the United Kingdom, was a central theme. The treatment of the failure of economics to encompass power as a factor determining changes in income distribution and of the way in which a maturing democracy can expand expectations and thereby threaten its own stability (Brittan) contributes fresh material on the central economic issue of inflation. An original insight into the mind of the arbitrator (Johnson) strikes a more optimistic note.

There is debate on regional policy and on Scotland's economic future, and on the past. 'The gap between Scottish and British employment and per capita income has narrowed and the unemployment relative has improved markedly with the result that emigration has decreased.' Mackay's description of the period since the early 1960s—which coincides with the most active regional policy—contrasts with the view that regional policy has failed (Simpson). On Scotland's economic future agreement seems closer: 'the 1970s are a turning point in which Scotland enters a new phase ... (in which) its rate of growth will increase relative to that of England and other countries of Western Europe' (Simpson); '(oil offers) a possible escape from the depressing economic record of Scotland over the last half century' (Mackay). The gap widens again, however, when the relationship between political structure and economic prosperity is discussed: 'the need to keep the "British economy" intact looks less attractive now than ever before' (Kellas) or 'The spill-over effects of English and Welsh decisions on Scotland and of Scottish decisions on England and Wales ... (are) great and the inefficiencies which could arise from entirely separate decision-making ... require some permanent system of communication, consultation and joint decision-taking, some central authority in other—less fashionable—words' (Alexander).

Debate was not confined to the economics and politics of nationalism. Qualified support for large-scale industrial units (Townsend) contrast sharply with the view that 'the adoption of smaller-scale technology could contribute enormously to the quality of life' (Bannock). Although both these contributors discussed size within the context of change, one leans towards economic growth as the outcome of change and the other towards the quality of life as its proper objective. It is fascinating to note how a sociologist (Eldridge) discussing organisation and change puts minimal emphasis on scale and concentrates on the complexity of organisations, distinguishing their several separate dimensions as technical, human, social, formal, informal and ideological. How well this contrast illustrates the point made in another paper: 'We (economists) must avoid the over-simplification that comes from using a crude economic variable to stand for complex social forces outside our comprehension' (Denton). The argument that in circumstances where increasing industrial scale appears inevitable it is necessary to develop special skills in 'the management of size', in which skills in human relations must play a major part (Scholey) illustrates an alternative approach to the problems of 'bigness'.

It was hardly to be expected that discussion of such extensive themes by social scientists from varying disciplines would produce unanimity, although the areas of agreement were more numerous than this brief introduction suggests. What can be claimed is that the topics chosen provided a fruitful focus for the socio-political economy approach. Both the strengths and weaknesses of this particular excursion underline the case for developing and extending this approach.

Strathclyde University
December 1974

K. J. W. ALEXANDER

Concepts and Methods

1

The Economic Contradictions of Democracy*

Samuel Brittan†

1 The Conjecture

The conjecture to be discussed here is that liberal representative democracy suffers from internal contradictions,[1] which are likely to increase in time; and, on present indications, the system is likely to pass away within the lifetime of people now adult.

The thesis itself has now become commonplace;[2] and any interest it has must lie in the supporting argument. There is no such thing as historical inevitability: and if my reasoning has any elements of validity, it may help to suggest either what can be done to improve the prospects for our type of democracy; or if that cannot be saved, what can be done to ensure that any successor form of government does the minimum of damage to more fundamental values.

In my own case the values which serve as a yardstick are those of an Open Society, where a large weight is put on both freedom of speech and freedom to choose one's own way of life, in which no group is oppressed or denied the means of subsistence, and in which the use of force and infliction of pain (whether or not dignified by the name of punishment) is reduced to the feasible minimum. I mention these clichés simply as a reminder of the more basic ends which any political system should serve. On balance, democracy has advanced them; but there is nothing necessary or invariable about the connection.

The two endemic threats to liberal representative democracy are (a) the generation of excessive expectations; and (b) the disruptive effects of the pursuit of group self-interest in the market place.

The two threats have different origins. Excessive expectations are generated by the democratic aspects of the system. The disruptive effects of group self-interest arise from elementary economic logic and are not directly connected with the political structure.

* A revised version of this Paper containing more supporting data can be found in the *British Journal of Political Science*, April 1975.
† Nuffield College, Oxford, and the *Financial Times*.

The 'liberal' aspect of liberal representative democracy is important as an inhibition on tackling the group pursuit of market power. Both People's Democracies and some trigger-happy military dictatorships have shown that they can deal at a price with the union problem, as well as with other group conflicts. (They do not always do so.) But it has yet to be shown that a society where legislation can only be enforced if it enjoys at least the tacit long run acceptance of all major groups, including those on the losing side, can do so. The omens are not good.

There are clear interrelations between the two problems of the pursuit of group self-interest and the generation of excessive expectations in the political market place. The unions—and other groups too—have not in the past made use of their full potential power. but have tended to make increasing use of it as time has passed. It is commonplace to observe that the size of group demands depends on members' expectations; but these in turn have been fanned by the competitive wooing of the electorate. Moreover, as already implied, liberal democracy inhibits governments from tackling group power either by an abnegation of the full employment commitment, or by the effective restriction of union monopoly power or the enforcement of an 'incomes policy',

A formula which may link the two problems is that *an excessive burden is placed on the sharing out function of government.*[3] There are incompatible expectations about what Government can do for people through regulation, expenditure and taxation; and a successful 'incomes policy' to secure full employment without currency collapse runs up against the demands of different groups for incompatible relative shares.

There is nothing uniquely British in the tensions described. But the fact that they are particularly acute in this country is shown by the use of the label 'English sickness' when they turn up elsewhere. In what follows, I shall take the UK as a case study without implying that the denouement will be either the same or different in other places.

2 The Political Market Place

To carry the analysis any further, it is necessary to put forward some view, inevitably brief and oversimplified, of the nature of liberal representative democracy.

The 'liberal' part of the label refers to the standard civil liberties of expression, association and assembly—together with the generally accepted constraints upon the degree of coercion which the forces of government can impose upon dissidents. I have in mind not some ideal free or open society[4] but the degree of tolerance and personal freedom which Western countries normally expect to achieve and lapses from which give rise to criticism and anxiety.

A good deal more needs to be said about the 'representative democracy' aspects of the system. My starting point is Schumpeter's theory. Schumpeter defined democracy as an *institutional arrangement in which individuals acquire the power to make political decisions by means of a competitive struggle for the people's votes.*[5]

There is a link between the 'liberal' and the 'democratic' aspects of the system thus defined, but it is a loose one. If rival political teams are to compete, a minimal freedom of debate is required; and once freedom has acquired a toehold in the party political arena it tends to spread to wider areas. Yet it is essential to remember the distinction between the two aspects. The link is loose enough to allow persecution of unpopular minorities and widespread restraints upon freedom of action in systems with unfettered elections and majority decisions. Indeed such repressive actions have been common, but less widespread (in modern times at least) than in undemocratic regimes.

The point of Schumpeter's theory becomes clear when we compare it with the popular theory[6] which assumes that electors have definite beliefs about policy, represented by political parties which are expected to implement them. Edmund Burke defined a political party as a group of men who intend to promote the public welfare upon some principles upon which they are all agreed. In subsequent forms of the popular theory, parties were actually expected to formulate their policies in response to the desires of their mass membership.

Such models of democracy received a body blow when nineteenth-century writers such as Michels, Mosca and Pareto showed that no mass democracy could or did work this way. Policies were formulated by small groups within political parties or the Civil Service; and what was done often had very little relation to professed ideologies. These sceptical conclusions were confirmed very much later by sophisticated opinion studies which showed that most voters were largely oblivious of the policy debates in Parliament and the Press. Changes in political allegiance were shown to be performance-related rather than issue-related. In other words, voters attempted to judge success in the pursuit of generally agreed objectives such as peace or prosperity rather than to evaluate rival objectives or alternative policies for achieving agreed objectives.

Not merely did they not use the labels 'left' or 'right': they simply did not think in such terms. To the extent that ordinary voters thought in terms of issues at all, their attitudes were largely atomistic. On many issues on which the official positions of the parties were sharply divided, the proportion of people supporting different policies bore almost no relation to partisan allegiance. The clusters or 'ideologies', linking together opinions on different issues among the politically interested minority, were almost completely absent among the mass electorate. Such refusal to conform to stereotype was due not to noncomformist heresy, but much more often to basic ignorance of the simplest facts taken for granted even in the most popular of newspapers or television programmes.[7] Only 50 per cent of one representative sample were consistent in opposing or supporting further nationalisation in three interviews in 1963-6. This was shown to be due to 'mere uncertainty of response' and not to genuine attitude changes. Voters simplify the problems of choice by shifting attention from policies to consequences—beliefs in the latter are formed by 'simple inferences from who is or was in power'.

Schumpeter's achievement was to show that representative democracy could work and need not be a fraud, despite these features. The best way to thing of politicians, he maintained, was neither as ideologues nor as spokesmen but as entrepreneurs who deal in votes just as oilmen deal in oil. The principles or policy planks which characterise a political party may be important for its success at a given moment, but they have no deeper or more permanent significance than the particular brands that a department store finds it expedient to carry this month but may well want to change next spring or autumn. Different department stores will feel more at home with different kinds of merchandise, but all will alter their lines in trial and error fashion in a bid to win public support. More deep-seated divergences are to be viewed as pathological symptoms.

Like all good theories, this is an unrealistic over-simplification. But it is neither as cynical nor a shocking as it appears at first sight. It is the political equivalent of Adam Smith's doctrine that it is not from the benevolence of the butcher, the brewer or the baker that we expect our dinner, but from their regard to their own interest. In politics as in economics, the pursuit of self-interest may, contrary to what unreflective moralists suppose, serve to promote the welfare of one's fellow citizens. Both the political and the economic markets are, of course, highly imperfect, although it is easier to analyse the imperfections than to suggest improvements.

The main advantage of Schumpeter's theory, however, is that it explains many phenomena which look puzzling or pathological on the basis of the classical theory. To begin with, it provides a criterion for distinguishing democracy from other systems in large societies where direct democracy is impossible. The people cannot rule in the USA or Britain any more than in the USSR, Chile or China. On the other hand, a monarch, despot, or dictator may enjoy majority support for his actions. It is the competitive bidding for votes among an extensive electorate that distinguishes the democratic system, not popular support for the regime.

The competitive theory can explain why the policies of the leadership of the main parties are likely to resemble each other far more than partisan enthusiasts would like; and why a party's policies may change so as to become almost unrecognisable in a very few years. It also explains the role of political leadership. The fact that most electors have in Schumpeter's words, at best an 'indeterminate bundle of vague impulses loosely playing about given slogans and mistaken impressions' is not fatal if the job of the elector is to choose between competing teams. Policy formulation is on this model a task for politicians and officials; and if the electorate does not like the result, it does not buy it again. It also explains the development of quasi-presidential tendencies in parliamentary systems, and why MPs on the winning side are often driven by the man they originally elected as leader. When democracy is working at its best, electorates or MPs may be presented with results which they welcome but which would never have occurred to them in the first place.

3 Non-Fatal Weaknesses

Schumpeter did not believe that either economic or political markets produced ideal results; which was not, of course, a condemnation. Some of the defects of democracy which he listed have become familiar platitudes; and not all require the Schumpeterian model to explain. What is striking is that they were identified in a book that first appeared in 1942. He gave pride of place to *the wastage of governmental energies*. Prime Ministers and their principal colleagues are involved in a never-ending contest—which goes on in only slightly less acute form between elections. Both their opponents and their own flock have to be watched carefully if the leaders are to remain in the saddle. A very small fraction of a Prime Minister's time is available for thinking about policy, or plain reflection.

Good political tactics do not always produce good policies. Because every issue is seen in the context of a constant partisan struggle, it becomes distorted. Short run ends, such as keeping the mortgage rate down, prevail over longer term aims, such as producing a sensible housing or credit policy. Whether or not adver-

tising or other mass media men are employed, their approach comes
to dominate. In other words, emotive catchphrases and reiterated
slogans or assertions count more in the public arena than logical
argument. The trouble is not so much that ordinary voters—who do
not and cannot rule—think in these terms, but that the political
professionals come to do so as well.

There is also the problem of product quality. The attitudes and
abilities that make for a good candidate are not necessarily those
of a good MP; and a good MP is not necessarily a good Minister.
Above all there is the danger that the political process may repel
men who could make a success of anything else. In view of all these
problems, Schumpeter was quite sure that politicians could not run
the economy—from which he did *not* draw the conclusion that
socialism was impossible, for reasons to be discussed later.

Other defects have emerged from subsequent work on the competitive model, such as that of Anthony Downs.[8] There is the
possible oppression of a minority by a bare majority, or of the
majority by a coalition of minorities with strong views on particular
issues. Special interest groups are likely to prevail over more
general interests, because of the concentration of the former and
dispersion of the latter. The beneficial impact of any one protectionist or restrictionist measure on an individual via his professional
or geographical interest is far greater than any loss he may bear
along with 50 or 60 million other citizens. The contrast is often
drawn between consumers and producers, but it can just as well
arise among different consumers. The beneficial impact on a home
purchaser of special subsidies or reliefs is felt far more sharply than
the general loss he bears through the tax-cost of these measures
along with all other taxpayers, including rentpayers and those who
have already paid for their own houses.

The case for liberal democracy, as it actually works, has been
unnecessarily undermined by the 'pluralist' writers, who for so long
dominated the American academic political scene, and who regarded
the 'log-rolling' bias of the system as a strength rather than a weakness. They made the mistake of assuming that if there were a fair
balance between business and labour interests, and between different
regions and industries, all would be well. Indeed they regarded the
clash of interest groups as itself part of the working of the benefi-
cent Invisible Hand.

It has not been difficult for academic radicals to show that some
interests are more effectively represented than others and that
citizens of higher status and wealth are both more prominent inside
the pressure groups and have easier access to them. From this they
have implied that Western Democracy is a sham and have hinted

that direct action or some unspecified form of revolution is to be welcomed. But the fundamental weakness of the pluralist position (which on this side of the Atlantic is represented by exponents of the 'Corporate State') would still exist even if every citizen belonged to a pressure group and exercised the same amount of power in this group. Nor would things be different if every consumer were also a producer and every recipient of a special subsidy also a taxpayer. For although a businessman, or trade unionist, or consumer of a particular product, may gain more then he loses from his own special favour, privilege or subsidy, he is likely to lose out on balance from the sum total of restrictions and distortions in all spheres combined.

As Mancur Olson has put it:

> Even if a pressure group system worked with perfect *fairness* for every group, it would still tend to work *inefficiently*. If every industry is favoured, to a fair or equal degree, by favourable government policies obtained through lobbying, the economy as a whole will tend to function less efficiently, and every group will be worse off than if none, or only some of the special interest demands had been granted. Coherent, rational policies cannot be expected from a series of *ad hoc* concessions to diverse interest groups.[9]

Pressure group politics of the old-fashioned log-rolling type (as distinct from withdrawing an essential service from the market place and using coercion to keep out substitute supplies) is, however, unlikely to be fatal to the success of democracy. Casual historical observation suggests that democracies can carry on almost indefinitely subsidising prestige high technology activities such as aerospace, protecting inefficient farmers, imposing tariffs and quotas, encouraging union restrictive practices, rigging interest rates for favoured groups, 'supporting' key prices—from air or cab fares to beef and beetroot—preserving monopoly rights for state industries, and carrying out hosts of similar welfare-reducing actions, without producing catastrophic results or even preventing a considerable advance in living standards.

4 Excessive Expectations

Schumpeter's own criterion for the success of a political system was fairly modest. By success he did not mean achieving an ideal, being on a Pareto optimum or anything of that kind, but simply that it

B

could reproduce itself without creating conditions which led to resort to undemocratic methods, or—which he took to be equivalent—that all major interests would in the long run abide by the results of the democratic process.

He himself was non-committal on democracy's prospects. But his own analysis provides plenty of grounds to expect a trend towards excessive expectations, which could indeed prove fatal. He drew here on some of the earlier analyses of crowd psychology. People in a crowd are apt to exhibit a reduced sense of responsibility and lower level of energy and thought than the same individuals in their private or business life. A crowd does not mean a screaming mob in a sultry city. It can just as easily be a television audience, or electorate, or a committee of generals in their 60s. Even supposedly individual demands are not the outcome of rational deliberation about the best means of satisfying inherent desires but can be artificially generated by advertising or propaganda.

These anti-rational or non-rational influences are less important in personal, business or professional life than in political behaviour. Frequently repeated experience in everyday life, as well as personal responsibilities, exert a rationalising influence. 'The picture of the prettiest girl that ever lived will in the long run prove powerless to maintain the sales of a bad cigarette.'[10] Failure to take this on board accounts for the vast overemphasis by Galbraith on the powers of a large firm to manipulate consumer demand.

The rationalising influence of personal experience can be extended to hobbies, relations with friends, the affairs of a small township or a small social group. Schumpeter concedes that it might also influence views on public policy where personal pecuniary matters are at stake. But here the influence acts mainly in favour of influencing short-run rationality and short-run aims. His most telling comparison is that of the attitude of the lawyer to his brief, to the same lawyer's attitude to political statements in his newspaper. In the first place he has not only the competence, but also the stimulus to master the material. In the latter case he is 'not all there' morally or intellectually. Without the pressures that come from personal responsibility, masses of information and education will not help, and he 'will not apply the canons of criticism he knows so well how to handle in his own sphere'. For most people the great political issues are 'sub-hobbies' to which they devote less attention than to bridge; and there is little check either on dark urges or on bursts of generous indignation.

The analysis of rational political behaviour leads to the conclusion that it is irrational to be too rational, because of the information and other costs involved. This is highlighted by the problem of the *voting paradox*, that is the problem of finding a self-interested motive for voting when the probability of any one vote determining the outcome is vanishingly small. Its importance is not the literal one of explaining why 70–80 per cent of electors vote. The cost of so doing is extremely small; and a sense of public duty, emotional satisfaction or a blow-up sense of self-importance can be called in aid. The validity of the phenomenon to which it refers can be seen by the way in which the slightest increase in the cost of voting, such as the possibility of missing a popular television programme, influences the turnout and extreme anxiety of the party leaders, especially those of the working-class party, to minimise all rival distractions.

The main point is that if a self-interested citizen has little or no incentive to vote, he has even less to make a detailed study of facts, controversies and policies. Any short cut, such as taking on trust views of the party one generally supports, or going by television impressions, will be quite rationally undertaken to avoid time-consuming study, which would in any case hardly be feasible over more than a very tiny range. Given the likely extent of individual influence, it is perfectly reasonable to regard political programmes as show business to be watched only if they are entertaining.

Nor is such reasoning applicable just to non-political citizens. An individual MP has such a small chance of influencing his party's policy that it is rational for him to use short-cut methods, such as following a particular leader of faction within his party, on all except a handful of issues of which he has made a speciality. It is on these lines that one can best explain the role of stereotyped packages of ideas, or ideologies. A politician, civil servant or academic who has neither the time nor the incentive to study every subject in depth can reasonably ask: 'From what stable does this particular idea come'? It may be better than going by pure hunch.

These considerations would not themselves be a threat to democracy if they simply led to the wrong result in particular elections or in particular policy decisions. Schumpeter's theory of democracy is designed so as not to depend on the existence of an informed electorate or even an informed Parliament. The trouble is *the lack of a budget constraint among voters*. This means that errors are biased in a particular direction. In their own private lives people know that more of one thing means less of something else, on a given income and capital. They know that they can improve the tradeoffs, such as that between take-home pay and leisure, by a careful choice of residence. But they also know that such improvements are not unlimited and cost effort to find. In the absence of such knowledge in the political sphere, electorates tend to expect too much from government action at too little cost, e.g. a painless improvement in economic growth or reduction in inflation, and they tend both to praise and blame governments for things which are largely outside their control. The impetus to consistency, without the discipline and responsibility of personal experience, is not strong.

The temptation to encourage false expectations among the electorate becomes overwhelming to politicians. The Opposition parties are bound to promise to do better and the Government party must join in the auction—explaining away the past, and outbidding its rivals for the future, whether by general hints or detailed promises. However cynical voters are about promises, their demands from government action and their attribution to it of responsibility for their own or the nation's past performance is altogether excessive. The analogy with commercial advertisements, which promise to fulfil all our daydreams if we buy 'getaway' petrol or the right type of underwear is inescapable; the difference is the absence of the immediate and personal corrective experience. The elector cannot compare experimentally a wide range of different governments and policies and examine their effects in isolation from other disturbing influences. Moreover, the normal competitive processes tend to bring to the top within each party leaders who genuinely believe that they can improve the tradeoffs more than is actually possible—usually by some form of minor improvement in machinery or administration. This is perfectly compatible with a great deal of apparent tough talking, but does not suit the sceptic or realist who actually knows the score.

The expectations that are relevant are not all the wants and demands that people make of life, but only those expectations which they expect the political process to underwrite. I am not pretending, of course, to offer a complete theory of political expectations, which are determined by innumerable forces apart from competitive vote-bidding. The spread of information about other people's life styles through the media and advertising, so that they look like attainable ideals rather than fantasies, is frequently cited. The breakdown of traditional ideas of hierarchy, which will be discussed below, is another obvious influence. It has also been suggested that expectations tend to be low during protracted periods of economic hardship; the gap between expectation and reality is greater during periods of prosperity and advance, and perhaps greatest of all when expectations are frustrated by a sudden and unexpected check to progress.[11] The main point to stress is that democracy, viewed as a process of political competition, itself imparts a systematic upward bias to expectations and compounds the other influences at work.

Is it possible that the gap between expectations and performance will ultimately prove self-correcting as public credibility becomes eroded? There are certainly periods of masochistic reaction in which parties vie with each other in promising hard times ahead. The periodic revulsions towards 'sweat, toil and tears' are, however, no more rational than the conventional outbidding. Each person is concerned that others should bear their proper share of sacrifice and that 'less essential' activities should be cut down to size. It is still likely that if we could add up the demands by different people for their own groups and their own favoured section of public expenditure, the result would still far exceed the resources available.

It is interesting, too, that moves away from excessive promises have so far taken the form only of hesitation about promising a larger cake. The outbidding continues on promises about distribution. Unfortunately, neither promises of redistribution from politicians, nor demands for it from the electorate, carry with it a knowledge of how much there is to redistribute, let alone a consensus on a just distribution. The elector tends, because he has no yardstick in his everyday life against which to measure consistency, to favour all worthy objects at the same time: more of the national income for the old and sick, the lower paid, the skilled craftsman, for those doing important professional work, the mortgagee, the rate-payer, and so on. The one group which people always think too well paid are the politicians, from whom omnipotence and omniscience are expected.

Nor are distribution and growth *per se* the only sphere in which excessive demands are made from the political process. The US Administration is expected to prevent pollution without increasing transportation or energy costs, protect forests and lower timber prices—and in general to protect the environment—without paying any obvious price. What has gone is the tacit belief in limiting the role of political decision; and this is likely to put a burden on democratic procedures which they are not designed to bear. The usefulness of inflationary finance as a short-term method of postponing political choice between incompatible objectives, enormously important though it may be, is but a particular case of consequences of inconsistent expectations and demands.

5 The Rivalry of Coercive Groups

It has already been suggested that the pursuit of self-interest through coercive means in the market place is a much more serious threat to democracy than the traditional log-rolling among legislators and Ministers. The most obvious form of this is the conflict of different groups of trade unionists—ostensibly with the Government or employers, but in reality with each other—for shares of the national product. This rivalry induces more and more sections of the population, including those who have previously relied on individualist efforts, into militant trade unionist attitudes in sheer self-defence.

The wage-push of rival unions forces government to choose between financing an inflationary level of wage settlements and facing a major increase in unemployment. Each group of union negotiators knows that all other groups are also pushing for wage increases; and the risk of its being left behind by the others is greater than the risk of the authorities refusing to finance the result. The employers on the other side of the table know this too. If we assume that the unions are not indefinitely fooled by 'money illusion', then the faster the rate of inflation the larger will be the money wage increases they will demand in an attempt to make sure of the real income their original settlements were intended to obtain. Thus as the process proceeds the result is not inflation, but accelerating inflation. In the last analysis the authorities have to choose between accepting an indefinite increase in the rate of inflation and abandoning full employment to the extent necessary to break the collective wage-push power of the unions.[12]

There have been numerous proposals, dating back in embryo to the 1944 White Paper, that demand management should seek to stabilise the growth of expenditure in money terms in line with the growth of productive potential. In that case the unions would know that the faster money wages rose the less jobs there would be. The same logic is inherent behind the principle of a fixed annual target for the growth of the money supply, and lay behind Peter Thorneycroft's pronouncements as Chancellor in the short period between his measures of September 1957 and his resignation over 'little local difficulties' early the following January.

The trouble with such policies is that they have only deterrent value; they might work if they carried credibility, but risk collapse if the threat had to be used. To take by no means fanciful illustrative figures. Let us imagine that a limit of 10 per cent per annum is set to the growth of nominal income and expenditure, but wage settlements, in conjunction with normal pricing procedures, require a growth of 20 per cent if unemployment is to be held constant and output to grow by a normal amount. What then is to be done? A reduction of output of nearly 10 per cent at the end of a single year of the policy, with whatever rise in unemployment that goes with it, will normally appear too large a price to pay. Until the spectre of hyperinflation and currency breakdown—perhaps disguised as a mammoth foreign exchange crisis—finally arrives, the monetary and fiscal targets will be the main ones to give way; and participants are well aware of this.

Union monopolies differ in an important way from other organised groups. A business monopoly, or cartel with market power, will hold its output below competitive levels for the sake of higher prices. A farmers' association will try to achieve the same effect by political lobbying. But none of these will normally withdraw output from the market until representatives of the public sign an agreement to pay more. This is a quasi-political power or threat, different in many ways from the textbook monopoly. Of course, there have been collective boycotts and even resorts to violence in business history, especially in the US in the late nineteenth century, but nothing as extended in scale or as pervasive throughout the economy as the effects of union power in the context of a commitment to full employment.

It is uncertain whether the unions are unique in the role they exercise. A possible comparison is the quadrupling of the oil price by the OPEC countries in 1973–4. If this was a once-for-all event, the analogy does not hold. For however severe the initial disruption, it could not push the world monetary authorities into policies of continuously accelerating inflation. If on the other hand there are going to be further attempts by producers to push up the price of oil (relative to other commodities) by withholding supplies, or if similar cartels are to be formed among other primary producers, and if in turn industrial workers are going to strike in an attempt to preserve their relative share of world income, then the analogy will hold and the problem becomes the wider one of the explosive potentialities of certain means of pursuing group interest. On present evidence, however, the problem focuses on union power in an environment of high labour demand.

The argument stressed by Peter Jay[13] that 'free' collective bargaining, full employment and a usable currency are not in the long run mutually compatible has never been convincingly answered; nor his conjecture that a liberal democracy is unlikely to be able to abandon any one of the three.

The conventional answer is that a voluntary or statutory 'income policy' could modify collective bargaining to the extent required. Even if a long term statutory incomes policy could resolve this dilemma—and this is not the place to discuss whether it could and at what price—it is unenforceable for any extended period if democracy is to remain 'liberal' and violent means of coercion are not to be employed on dissenting groups. (Indeed if public opinion is in this sense 'liberal', then it is unenforceable so long as democracy of any sort prevails.)

Thus the only sort of incomes policy that could help would be a voluntary one, or at least a statutory one that enjoyed the 'full-hearted consent' of those affected by it. Apart from brief emergency freezes, the main problem posed by such a policy is one of relativities, as every schoolboy knows.

Agreement on such relativities is extremely unlikely on any self-interested basis. Wage restraint is a 'public good', which means that it is in the interest of each union group that other unions show a restraint while it goes out for as much as it can get itself. For it is clear to any particular union leader that most of the gains from price stability and fuller employment spill over to members of other unions and the general public, while the costs of settling for less than he could obtain are highly concentrated among his own members.

It is sometimes asserted that the explosive potentialities from the collective pursuit of self-interest are due to the new vulnerability of a modern economy to group action which did not previously exist. But it is often forgotten that as long ago as 17 July 1914, Lloyd George declared that if the threats of the Irish Rebellion and the Triple Industrial Alliance were to materialise, 'the situation will be the gravest with which any government has had to deal for centuries'. Ernest Bevin subsequently said of these events: 'It was a period which, if the war had not broken out would have, I believe, seen one of the greatest revolts the world would have ever seen.'

Indeed, the main problem facing the analysis so far presented is why the tensions discussed did not emerge much earlier. We have no lack of warnings about the self-destructive tendencies of democracy dating back well into the nineteenth century. Bagehot's Introduction to the Second Edition of the *English Constitution*, written after the 1867 Reform Bill, is full of gloomy forebodings about the effects of enfranchising an ignorant and greedy electorate, and full of fury with Disraeli for having sold the pass.

6 The Vanishing Heritage

A good insight into the forces by which liberal democracy has so far protected itself against the tensions proclaimed by the doom-mongers can be obtained by going back to Schumpeter and re-examining some of the conditions he set for the effective working of the system. The most important was that the *effective range of political decision should not be extended too far*. Most issues are too complex to be decided by a competitive vote-seeking process. Although Parliament may vote on such issues and Ministers may introduce the legislation, their actions are purely formal, as the real decisions will have been made elsewhere. This applies not only to issues such as the permissible size of the Budget deficit or official operations in the foreign exchange market, but to as fundamental a matter as the criminal code, which would otherwise be at the mercy of alternating fits of vindictiveness and sentimentality.

Schumpeter makes a very firm distinction between extending the area of state authority and extending the area of political decision. The former can be done by means of agencies, whose heads are not appointed by competition for votes and who do not have to please the electorate in any direct or immediate sense. Apart from the permanent Civil Service, there are many special agencies whose non-political nature is constantly stressed both by themselves and by the Government of the day. Perhaps the most interesting historical example is the pre-1914 Bank of England which made key economic policy decisions at its own discretion. There are numerous regulatory agencies in the US, which if they are influenced by anyone, are influenced by the industries they are supposed to regulate. In Britain we have long had experience of organisations such as the BBC, the University Grants Committee or the Morrisonian public corporation. It is no coincidence that bodies such as the PIB, the Pay and Prices Boards, or *ad hoc* committees presided over by judges, have been used to extend state control into the most sensitive areas of economic life.

Another vital condition put forward by Schumpeter for the success of a competitive vote-bidding system was *tolerance and democratic self-control*. All groups must be willing to accept legislation on the statute book. Political warfare must be kept within certain limits; and this involves the Cabinet and Shadow Cabinet being followed by their supporters and not being pushed from behind. Political action is to be left to politicians without too much back-seat driving, let alone direct action. We cannot expect to see these conditions unless the main interests are agreed on the broad structure of society. If the electorate is divided into two or more deeply hostile camps, or there are rival ideals on which no compromise is possible, these restraints will cease to function and democracy may wither.

A further requirement was *the existence of a well-trained bureaucracy*. Not the powerless eunuchs of constitutional mythology, but a group with their own principles not merely of procedure, but in a more subtle sense of policy as well, deciding on their own promotions, and enjoying security of tenure. Many people would say that we have such a class, which has been responsible for our major postwar blunders and for preventing both Labour and Conservative governments from implementing distinctive policies of their own;

and that this had led to a proliferation of ideas for introducing irregulars, outsiders, ministerial cabinets, 'think tanks' and so on, the results of which have been—to put it mildly—not spectacular.

The reason why an entrenched bureaucracy is so essential is precisely because politicians are professionals at dealing in votes, but amateurs both in administration and in policy-making, with a strong tendency (already discussed) to take refuge in the world of the advertising slogan and the media headline; in other words, the alleged orthodoxy and lack of imagination of the bureaucrat is part of the price of having a democratic system at all. An interesting straw in the wind is the current proposal that certain civil servants should be assigned the job of advising the Opposition, so that it does not come to office so ill-prepared. One very prominent official not long ago observed that he would like to be on holiday for the first two years after every change of Government.

But without the fulfilment of the earlier conditions—a limit on the area of political decision and a sufficient agreement on the broad structure of society to enable groups to accept legislation with which they disagree—such a professional bureaucracy will not function effectively and its morale and effectiveness will be undermined (as they manifestly have been in the UK since the mid-1960s).

Mass electorates were able to accept the Schumpeter conditions of self-restraint for a surprisingly long period partly because they were slow to realise their power. The lack of incentives for the voter to inform himself have already been emphasised. There were also a series of *ad hoc* events such as the First World War, which produced an external threat and a patriotic myth to override sectional conflicts, and then came the great Depression which weakened the market power of the trade unions.

But just as important was an ethic, which took a long time to erode which limited the demands on the sharing out functions of the state. As Kristol has emphasised,[14] personal success was seen by nineteenth-century defenders of capitalism as having a firm connection with 'duty performed'. In a society

> still permeated by a Puritan ethic [it] was agreed that there was a strong correlation between certain personal virtues—frugality, industry, sobriety, reliability, piety—and the way in which power, privilege, and property were distributed. And this correlation was taken to be the sign of a just society, not merely a free one. Samuel Smiles or Horatio Alger would have regarded Professor Hayek's writings [divorcing reward from merit] as slanderous of his fellow Christians, blasphemous of God, and ultimately subversive of the social order.

The point that Kristol does not bring out sufficiently is that the public morality of early capitalist bourgeois society was a transitional one. On its own grounds it could not hope to stand up to serious analysis. Luck was even then as important as merit in the gaining of awards, and merit was inherently a subjective concept in the eye of the beholder. Hayek is right not to base his defence of a market economy upon it. Early capitalist civilisation was living on the moral heritage of the feudal system under which each man had a superior to whom he owed obligations and from whom he received protection in a 'great chain of duties'. A medieval king was expected to 'do justice and to render each his due'. It was not a matter of what the king thought a subject ought to have, or what the subject thought best for himself, but what belonged to him according to custom, which in turn was supported by theological sanction.

For a long time capitalist civilisation was able to live on this feudal legacy, and the aura of legitimacy was transferred from the feudal lord to the employer, from the medieval hierarchy of position to that derived from the luck of the market place. But this feudal legacy was bound to be extinguished by the torchlight of secular and rationalistic inquiry, which was itself so closely associated with the rise of capitalism. The personal qualities of middle-class leaders did not help to kindle that affection for the social order which is probably necessary if it is not to be blamed for the inevitable tribulations and disappointments of most people's lives. Modern politicians and business chiefs lack the glamour of an aristocracy. With neither the trappings of tradition, nor the heroic qualities of great war leaders or generals, they cannot excite the identification or hero worship which previously reconciled people to much greater differences of wealth and position than exist today. Moreover, the 'fairer' the process of selection, the less the governing classes are differentiated by special clothes or accents, the more they will be resented. At most they are tolerated on the strict condition that they bring results; and we have seen that expectations here tend to be excessive.

Schumpeter himself had some half-hearted hopes that the degree of institutional consensus and agreement on fundamentals, required for the working of democracy, might be restored under 'socialism'. For one thing, the issue of capitalism versus socialism would be out of the way, and there would be no more argument about profits, dividends, private ownership of capital or gains from rising land values. Moreover, the twentieth-century development of non-political agencies made socialism possible and perhaps compatible with democracy. By socialism he had in mind the old-fashioned definition of collective control over the means of production, roughly the 'Clause 4' conception. But the condition of success was that democratic politics was *not* extended to economic affairs. Beyond setting the rules in the most general way possible, it was essential that politicians resist the temptation to interfere with the activities of the managers of state enterprises and regulatory boards. (He had in mind a form of market socialism on Lange-Lerner lines.) Indeed Schumpeter remarked that at long last managers would be able to do their jobs without guilt-feelings, and with more freedom not only from interfering politicians, but also from fussing committees of consumers, demands for workers' control and all other claims for 'participation'.

We do not, however, need to follow out these paradoxes, because the type of collectivism now in vogue among all parties concerns not only ownership of producing assets, but also, and more important, relative incomes. The popular desire is to transfer from the private to the public sphere the determination of who gets how much; and to make this determination neither on the basis of market values, nor egalitarian principles, nor some compromise between them, but by a revival of the medieval notion of the just wage—a doctrine sometimes miscalled 'fairness'. This is to be done moreover without benefit of the feudal relationships and scholastic theology which enabled an earlier age to attach a meaning to such concepts.

It is hardly conceivable that anything as sensitive as the determination of relative rewards will be left to bodies enjoying the degree of autonomy of the pre-1914 Bank of England, or the nationalised industries before their finances and freedom were undermined by prices and incomes policy. Reference has already been made to bodies such as the Pay Board which may occasionally provide politicians with a useful fig leaf. But if pre-tax incomes are to be determined, or even heavily influenced, by state authority, elected politicians will want—quite rightly—to have the last word; and their decisions are bound to figure prominently in the competitive struggle for votes, again rightly so. Thus currently fashionable doctrines, so far from providing a solvent for the tensions of democracy, seems likely to make them worse.

To sum up so far. The best way of making sense of democratic political practice is to see it as a competition for power by means of votes among competing teams. Even viewed in this relatively unambitious light, it is subject to endemic and growing weaknesses, the chief of which are the generation of excessive expectations and the disruptive effects of the pursuit of group self-interest. This weakness is aggravated by the lack of any widely shared belief in the legitimacy of either the present order or of any feasible alternative social order in which democracy might operate.

7 The Mirage of 'Social Justice'

It should by this time be obvious that a resolution of the problems of liberal democracy is unlikely on a basis relying entirely on self-interest or private interest (which need not be selfish in the vulgar sense). Can any other motives be brought in which would both make members of economic groups refrain from exercising their full market power and induce electors to reduce the excessive and incompatible demands they make on government services? Is it possible to create or evolve a consensus, so far missing, on a legitimate social order which would appeal to people's sense of justice and persuade them to moderate their pursuit of private interest, both in the ballot box and in their other collective activities?

The problems discussed would clearly be a good deal if there was some consensus on how goods, status and power should be shared out. The common view that the basis of consent at present missing could be supplied by the pursuit of 'social justice' or 'fairness' is in all probability fallacious. At its most primitive level such thinking assumes that 'social justice' and 'fairness' are natural qualities such as redress or hardness, which are either present or not. Some more sophisticated exponents of this approach realise the subjective nature of such concepts and try to seek a *de facto* consensus. But there is in fact little agreement on what *ought* to determine relative income levels, let alone wider matters of power, opportunity, prestige or influence.[15] As a leading sociologist has written: 'Given the diversity of moral positions that are tenable in the existing state of public opinion, virtually any occupational group seeking a pay increase is likely to be able to find some legitimisation for pressing its case.'[16] Hence the proliferation of incompatible criteria: rewarding skill, overcoming labour shortages, helping the lower paid, preserving traditional differentials and so on.

There are two logically tenable ways of looking at the distribution of resources. One is to see it as a pie to be divided up by a central authority. From this point of view, the natural principle of division is equality and departures from it have to be justified. The other is to emphasis that

> we are not in the position of children who have been given some portions of pie ... There is no central distribution. What each person gets, he gets from others who give it to him in exchange

for something, or as a gift. In a free society, diverse persons control different resources, and new holdings arise out of the voluntary exchange and actions of persons ... The total result is the product of many individual decisions.[17]

Provided that the initial holdings were justly acquired, there can be no question of social injustice or wrongful distribution—although there may still be a desire to help the worst off for humanitarian reasons.

The two approaches may be called the entitlement theory and the pie theory. The weakness of the entitlement theory is that the very content of property rights and the rules governing their transfers, as well as their physical protection, are the result of collectively enforced rules and decisions, which we are at liberty to change. As Froude put it: 'Without the State there would be no such thing as property. The State guarantees to each individual what he has earned ... and fixes the conditions on which this protection will be granted.'[18] The weakness of the pie theory is that there is no fixed sum to go round, that individuals add to the pie by their activities (the success of which may be very imperfectly correlated with effort, let alone merit), and it is by no means obvious that others should treat the results as part of a common pool. Both the pie and the entitlement theories have elements of validity, but there is no obvious compromise between them, which is likely to be either logically or emotionally satisfying.

The equality suggested by the pie theory is, of course, notoriously difficult to define. Is it to be equality in relation to individuals, or families, or needs? Is someone with greater capacity for happiness to be given more, as in some versions of utilitarianism, or less to compensate for his inborn advantage? These complications are endless; and they are multiplied enormously once we abandon absolutes and talk about 'more equality' or 'less inequality'. The essential point has, however, been well stated by Bertrand de Jouvenel: 'Every allocation of reward' which is founded 'on equality under a certain aspect, will be hierarchical and contrary to equality under another aspect'.[19]

Most popular discussion of relativities, 'national job evaluation' and similar motions, are based neither on the pie nor on the entitlement theory, but on the very slippery idea of reward according to moral merit. The argument against this has been well stated by F. A. Hayek, who points out that even if all inherited wealth or differences in educational opportunity could be abolished, there would still be no inherent moral value attaching to the resulting distribution of income and wealth.

The inborn as well as the acquired gifts of a person clearly have a value to his fellows which does not depend on any credit due to him for possessing them. There is little a man can do to alter the fact that his special talents are very common or exceedingly rare. A good mind or a fine voice, a beautiful face or a skilful hand, a ready wit or an attractive personality are in a large measure as independent of a person's efforts as the opportunities or experiences he has had. In all these instances the value which a person's capacities or services have for us and for which he is recompensed has little relation to anything that we can call moral merit or deserts.[20]

Indeed it is one of the advantages of a market economy enjoying basic bourgeois liberties that a man's livelihood does not depend on other people's valuation of his merit. It is sufficient that he should be able to perform some work or sell a service for which there is a demand. Hayek concedes that as an organisation grows larger it will become inevitable that ascertainable merit in the eyes of managers (or some conventional seniority structure) should determine rewards. But so long as there is no one single organisation with a comprehensive scale of merit, but a multiplicity of competing organisations with different practices (as well as smaller organisations and a self-employed sector), an individual still has a wide degree of freedom and choice.

Hayek is, however, wrong to suppose that all policies for redistribution of income and wealth inevitably involve assessing merit, measuring need, or aiming to achieve equality of reward—whatever the latter would mean. There is another position. This is to accept the rankings of the actual, or a reformed market, but to use fiscal means to narrow differentials so that the game is played for smaller stakes. What is then needed is a view on the *general shape* of a tolerable distribution which does not involve a moralistic evaluation of any person or occupation.

One of the interests of Professor John Rawl's theory of justice[21] is that although he agrees with Hayek that reward based on supposed merit is neither desirable nor feasible, he nevertheless believes that the concept of social justice can be given a definite meaning. Rawls attempts to introduce an element of impartiality into the assessment of distribution by means of the 'veil of ignorance'. The idea is to work out the principles on which 'free and rational persons concerned to further their own interests' would desire their community to be run if they did not know their own social or economic place, the market value of their own talents, and many other key features of their real situation. A wealthy man might

like to establish principles which minimise taxes for welfare purposes; a poor man might espouse principles of an opposite kind. If
one excludes knowledge of one's own actual situation, there is some
chance of working out the principles on a disinterested basis.

The Rawls theory is the most ambitious and serious modern
attempt to construct a theory of social justice, which neither attempts
to assess merit nor to aim at complete equality, but nevertheless
seeks to provide criteria for state action in the field of income
distribution and elsewhere. The 'maximin' principle, in which
inequalities are justified if, and only if, they are to the advantage of
the least well off, is at bottom a sophisticated version of the pie
theory designed to take into account the effects of slicing on the
size of the pie. Yet, at least according to my reading of the critical
literature, it has not succeeded.

The basic flaw in the argument[22] is the belief that a thought
process under the 'veil of ignorance' must yield a unique result,
and the consequent attempt to erect a dubious system of orderings
and priorities which has kept the academic industry fully employed,
if not 'overheated'. The 'veil of ignorance' is a very useful device
for narrowing the range of disagreement, despite the imaginative
leap required; but it cannot eliminate differences in subjective
preferences. The varying hypothetical distributions which different
people would support under the 'veil of ignorance', would reveal
differences in attitudes to uncertainty. Someone with a taste for
gambling would be interested in seeing that there were some really
big incomes, just in case he came out lucky. One might hazard the
guess that if they were ignorant of their own position in the income
distribution, most people would be concerned to 'level up' at the
bottom so that there was no longer a depressed minority to which
they might be consigned. Attitudes would, however, still differ a
great deal towards the number and height of the summits at the
upper end of the incomes distribution. Rawls himself agrees that
even if his principles are accepted, there is much room for disagreement about the range of social and economic inequalities they
actually justify.

Apart from the purely logical difficulties, it is doubtful if the
Rawls scheme would ever have much popular appeal. A criticism
which would probably be echoed by non-philosophers and non-
economists, if they were following the discussion is that, starting off
as it does, from calculations of rational self-interest, the Rawls
theory contains very little 'justice' in the sense in which that word is
normally used. Irving Kristol has pointed to the huge gap between
Hayek's concept of a 'free society', in which we do not claim that
position and reward depend on merit or work, and the traditional

defences of capitalism, which asserted that they did.[23] But the contrast is equally great with social democracy of the Rawls type based purely on what 'free and rational persons' might contract to do in their own self-interest.

Thus if it is true that people do have, as Kristol argues, an emotional yearning for some quasi-theological justification for differences in position, power or well-being; if the rational arguments for accepting a system that does not aim at complete distributive justice are too abstract or sophisticated to command assent; and if there is an emotional void that cannot be met merely by rising incomes and humanitarian redistribution unrelated to 'merit', then the outlook for liberal democracy is a poor one.

8 Further Perspectives

One obvious gap in the preceding pages has been any specific scenario by which liberal democracy might disappear; and I have deliberately avoided discussing questions such as: 'Could the army become a political agency' or 'What form might a middle-class revolt take'? The view that the present situation is unsustainable does not itself imply anything about the process of change or the nature of any new system.

There is no need to suppose that there will be an overnight coup; there could be a gradual process of disintegration of traditional political authority and the growth of new sources of power. Indeed, a continuation of present trends might lead to a situation where nothing remained of liberal democracy but its label. Nor need we assume that a new system will be repressive but efficient. It is just as easy to imagine a combination of pockets of anarchy combined with petty despotism, in which many of the amenities of life and the rule of law are absent, but in which there are many things which we will be prevented from doing or saying. Nor can we say whether the union problem will be tackled by right-wing authoritarian measures or by the unions themselves becoming the agents of repression in a People's Democracy. Let us not forget too that authoritarian regimes have their own weaknesses—above all those arising from the lack of effective criticism; and nothing that has been said in this Paper implies that they will provide a stable solution.

Above all, diagnosis is not historical prophecy. My conjecture about democracy could be forestalled by events or by preventive action. This is, after all the point of making it. To point to weaknesses, tensions and dangers does not mean that we must succumb to them.

C

It would be presumptuous to add a 'blueprint for salvation' as a tailpiece or afterthought. In any case, the key to a more hopeful future lies in understanding rather than in blueprints. The most popular nostrum at the time of writing is a coalition or 'Government of National Unity'. Its advantage would be that it might do something about the generation of excessive expectations. If the leaders of the main parties shared responsibility, it would be difficult to pretend that all national difficulties spring from the 'other side' being in power and that all would be well if there were a change of government.

The big disadvantage of a coalition is that it would tend to represent the conventional wisdom and wishful thinking of the hour, which would be even more difficult to displace than it is at present. Moreover, the process of outbidding could be eventually started up again by outside 'extremists', and disillusionment against all conventional politicians could eventually increase further. But there are occasions when it is worth buying time and I would stick to the judgement I made in 1968 that 'an experimental interval of coalition would be desirable'.[24]

Nor, while on the subject of buying time, should one overlook the possibility of a change of economic luck. A favourable combination of events such as improved terms of trade, followed by good fortune from North Sea oil, would provide a better climate for the 'sharing out' functions of Government than the last few years in which expectations of growth have suffered a nasty jolt, and economic policy has looked like a zero sum game between different sections.

Yet it would be folly to depend on such once-for-all palliatives to do more than postpone the tendency of liberal democracy to generate unfulfillable expectations or the tensions arising from the pursuit of group self-interest. As the tensions spring from attitudes, it is in the realm of attitudes that a more enduring solvent will have to be found. Even an authoritarian government would be ultimately dependent on opinion, although perhaps the opinion of fewer or different people. As David Hume remarked:[25]

> The governors have nothing to support them but opinion. The Sultan of Egypt or the Emperor of Rome might drive his harmless subjects like brute beasts, against their sentiments and inclination; but he must at least have led his mamelukes or praetorian bands like men by their opinion.

It is, of course, not an easy matter to say in complex societies whose opinion counts and to what extent.

There is one tempting blind alley to avoid. Some philosophic conservatives trace the source of the contemporary malaise to the abandonment of the belief in absolute values and look back with nostalgia to the time when no one supposed that ordinary people were the best judge of their own happiness, but it was taken for granted that such knowledge was available to a metaphysical, religious or political elite. Now even if this is true as a diagnosis, it offers little hope of cure. For myths cannot hope to serve a social purpose if people know that they are myths and seek to preserve them in a utilitarian spirit. If god does not exist, he cannot be invented.

Many of our present tensions would become much less important in the unlikely event of a genuine revulsion against materialism or the 'consumer society'. Modern technology does make it possible to reduce the obsession with procuring ever more material products, without having to submit to a life of ascetic poverty. It is unfortunate that the leadership among those who talk of an 'Alternative Society' should have been taken over by intolerant and envious political revolutionaries and that those most concerned with freedom, personal relations and the devising of new life styles for *themselves*, should have lost ground.

Differences in status, because they lie in the eye of the beholder, are potentially *both* more disruptive and more emollient than material differences. If there is general agreement on what the top status positions are, combined with an intense desire to be at the top and a resentment of the way that it is recruited, then a great deal of tension can be predicted. By contrast a society in which manual workers, professional and white-collar workers all regarded *themselves* as the true aristocrats, would be good for people's self-respect. While not everyone can occupy the top income brackets, it would be possible for most people to value highly the activities that they themselves do; and the greater the range of human qualities that were admired, the less there need be feelings of inferiority. There is no exact or necessary correspondence between income or position in the productive process, and either self-esteem or esteem in the eyes of others. But this is an area where opinion is all important, and Marxists who insist on a one dimensional model of satisfaction both help to make it true and increase the sum of human misery.

The ultimate sin of the politicians, academics and the media has been their obsession with interpersonal and intergroup comparisons. This is seen in concepts such as 'relative deprivation' in sociology, 'inequality' (a loaded way of describing differences), 'interdependent utilities' in economics, or 'equal freedom' in political philosophy. It is no use saying that resentment and envy of the

possessions and achievements of others, and strong views about
people's life-styles, simply exist, whether the liberal individualist
likes it or not. The attitudes in question are influenced by what is
said and written; and the contribution of the so-called intelligentsia
is to focus all attention on relativities to the exclusion of absolutes.
Moreover, their object in so doing is not to stir up personal rivalry
and emulation, which add to the interests and joys, as well as
unhappiness, of life; it is to emphasise differences while asserting
that they should not be there.

If comparisons are always with other people, and never with past
achievements, the hope of progress is at an end; and what the
pessimistic theologians have failed to do will have been achieved
by the secular egalitarians. If we look at definite things, such as
treatment of children, the level of nutrition, health, housing or
consumption of the poorest, or the efficiency and humanity of the
penal system, improvement is possible. In the realm of intangibles
such as self-respect and regard for others, improvement is more
difficult, but can still be envisaged; and this also applies to the
reduction of coercion in human affairs. But if all that matters is
whether other people are better or worse off than oneself in these
respects, then human history is a zero sum game. Even if the
principle of diminishing marginal utility is misapplied to assert that
the gains of those who move up are greater than the losses of those
who move down, then all advance stops when equality has been
reached; and as has already been pointed out, the definition of that
state is far from obvious and likely to cause extreme acrimony, with
most people feeling that they have been treated les equally than
others.

Quite apart from these conceptual difficulties, there is no reason
to suppose that any target reduction in 'inequality' (or even in the
share of property income) would supply a basis of consent to the
social or economic structure. Indeed, the more that policy concentrates on eliminating disparities and differentials, the greater the
sense of outrage likely to be engendered by those that remain.
Moreover, the smaller the financial contrast between the mass of
wage and salary earners and the wealthy minority, the greater the
attention that is likely to be paid to relativities among workers. As
it is, 90 per cent of consumer spending comes from wages, salaries
and social security payments, and the annual wage round is to a
large extent a contest between different groups of workers for
relative shares. It is one of the defects of the present preoccupation
with differentials, whether from a desire to establish an 'incomes
policy' or from a wish to iron out 'inequality', that each group
becomes much more keenly aware of what other groups are obtain-

ng and more critical of the basis of comparison, which can always
be made in more than one way; and this increases rather than
diminishes the ferocity of the struggle.

The ideal of equality has had a noble role in human history. It
has served to assert that all men and women are entitled to respect,
and to rally people against oppression. But it has now turned sour.
Liberal democracy will not be saved by detailed policy programmes
which will soon be overtaken by events. It could yet be saved of
contemporary egalitarianism were to lose its hold over the intelligentsia. But this will only happen if those who recognise it for the
disease it has become, are prepared to come out in the open and
have uncongenial labels placed upon them, as well as to consort
with strange bedfellows on whom a watchful eye will always have
to be kept.

Notes

1. Strictly speaking only statements can be contradictory, not events or
   procedures. The title of this paper represents a stretching of the term of
   the kind in which Marx indulged when speaking of the 'contradictions
   of capitalism'.
2. It had a little more novelty when I put forward an earlier version of
   this paper at a Nuffield Seminar at the beginning of 1974.
3. I am very much indebted to Bertrand de Jouvenel for suggesting this
   formulation.
4. My own view of what Western societies could and should attempt to
   achieve can be found in *Capitalism and the Permissive Society*,
   Macmillan, 1973.
5. *Capitalism, Socialism and Democracy*, London, 1954, Part IV.
6. Plamenatz is probably right to argue that the 'popular' theory of
   democracy is a better name than Schumpeter's own term 'classical'. *See
   Democracy and Illusion*, p. 39, 1973.
7. The *locus classicus view* of such studies is Angus Campbell *et al.*: *The
   American Voter*, New York, 1960. For the application to the UK, see:
   Butler and Stokes: *Political Change in Britain*, 1969 (second edition,
   1974), which provides the above illustration.
8. *An Economic Theory of Democracy*, New York, 1957.
9. *The Logic of Collective Action*, Harvard, 1965 and 1971, p. 174.
10. *Capitalism, Socialism and Democracy*, p. 263.
11. These influences are discussed in W. G. Runciman, *Relative Deprivation
    and Social Justice*, Penguin, 1972, Chapters 2 and 4.
12. I have analysed all this in greater detail in *Second Thoughts on Full
    Employment Policy*, Centre for Policy Studies, London, 1975.
13. In several articles in *The Times* in 1974.
14. Chapter 2, of *Capitalism Today* (ed. Bell and Kristol), Mentor Books,
    New York, 1971.

15. The important problems that would arise both for efficiency and for human freedom if there were an attempt to enforce a pattern of income differentials for different occupations, different from that of the market, are not discussed here. See: S. Brittan, *Capitalism and the Permissive Society*, Macmillan, 1973, pp. 103–9, and 124–40.
16. John Goldthorpe: 'Social Inequality and Social Integration in Modern Britain', in *Poverty, Inequality and Class Structure* (ed. Wedderburn), Cambridge, 1974.
17. Robert Nozick: 'Distributive Justice', *Philosophy and Public Affairs*, Fall 1973.
18. *Address to the Liberty and Property Defence League*, London, 1887.
19. *Sovereignty*, p. 151.
20. *The Constitution of Liberty*, Chapter 6.
21. *A Theory of Justice*, Oxford, 1972.
22. There are many other objections to the theory, not all pedantic quibbles, but some quite fundamental. See for instance: Brian Barry, *The Liberal Theory of Justice*, Oxford, 1973. R. M. Hare, *The Philosophical Quarterly*, April and July 1973. Kenneth J. Arrow, *Harvard Institute of Economic Research, Discussion Paper 287*, 1973 and Nozick, op. cit.
23. Op. cit.
24. *Left or Right*, Secker and Warburg, p. 166.
25. *Essay on the First Principles of Government*.

2

Economic Theory and Economic Growth

*Geoffrey Denton**

Philosophical discussions of methodology frequently conclude that economics, with other sciences, is impossible. Economists are attempting to measure the unmeasureable and to forecast the unpredictable. We need not concern ourselves with such philosophical dilemma, which arise out of the problem of judging what questions economics ought to be capable of answering. Some of the supposed failures of economics may not be failed answers but failed questions: over-ambition rather than under-performance. Natural science, despite its unquestioned achievement, also has difficulty in answering the difficult questions, such as the origin of the universe, or will it rain next week. Faced with this problem, however, any science must at least achieve clarity with respect to what are the questions it claims to be able to answer, both for the sake of its own internal coherence and in order to gain respect and influence with outsiders.

Sam Brittan has examined one important cause of our economic difficulties: the excessive expectations of electorates in a modern democracy. The purpose of my paper is to comment on some of the 'credibility' problems which arise for economic science with particular reference to the contribution of economic theory to growth policy and growth performance. I shall interpret the term 'theory' both widely and loosely to embrace those economic analyses that have been influential in forming policy in the United Kingdom during the last quarter century.

The first part of the paper will comment on theories more directly related to growth; dealing with investment, technology, labour supply, demand, external payments, and industrial restructuring. The second part will comment on the relevance to economic growth of theories not normally considered to have a very close connection,

* Reader in Economics, University of Reading.

dealing with resource allocation, income distribution, fluctuations international resource allocation, economic integration, and the regional distribution of economic activity.

Given this extremely broad canvas, it will be apparent that in a short paper only brief and selective comments can be made on each of the topics. Nevertheless, it is my thesis that an overall view of this kind is essential if we are to obtain a sensible appraisal of what economic theory has to offer in the way of determining policies for growth and influencing the growth performance of the economy.

Mathematical models of economic growth, attempting to clarify the contribution of the many variables determining the rate of growth have been numerous, but attempts to establish the quantitative influence of the many different variables on growth have failed for many reasons: including the difficulty of establishing agreed definitions and measures of the relevant variables, for example in the area the supply and quantity of labour, and the immense data problems encountered in econometric work. The most glaring deficiency of these models has been that the error term required to make the equations fit the observed growth has frequently been as important as all the known variables put together. 'Residual' factors in economic growth have been a fascinating topic, but since their interpretation has been a matter of rather subjective judgement, with economists variously choosing items such as technical improvements in production, education and the advance of knowledge, and expectations of future demand, there have been no firm conclusions on which policy could be safely based. While in general economists have been correspondingly modest in giving advice to governments on how to promote growth, they have on several occasions succumbed to the inevitable pressures from government (itself under pressure from electorates) and business to propose policies based on what they themselves have understood to be only reasonably plausible hypotheses.

Given the meagre results of the attempts to build ambitious general growth models, various partial models drawing attention to particular variables, have enjoyed a vogue at different times, and governments have in practice tended to base their policies on these.

Capital investment has probably enjoyed a more consistent popularity than any other variable in most countries, since a very simple equation: the proportion of national income invested, multiplied by the yield on investment, equals the rate of growth of national income: appears to lead to a clear prescription for raising the proportion of national income invested. Thus UK governments have been persuaded to give tax allowances or grants to encourage investment. The fact that the ratio of investment to national income remains among the lowest in advanced economies suggests that these measures have not been very effective. Among numerous snags, firms may accept the inducements but make no investments beyond those they would have made without them; other firms may be induced to make investments that are socially unproductive or unprofitable; incentives may be offset by the taxation required to pay for them; while unless technique can be improved, the scope for further investment is probably constrained by the availability of labour.

Awareness of the need to increase the productivity of investment, especially in an economy with a slow rate of growth of labour supply, led to parallel attempts to increase research and development. Investment incentives have been extended to this form of investment, but in addition more direct action, such as government financed research centres, grants to private industry, and the public provision of scientific education, have been used to improve British technology. But the efforts have in practice been concentrated on a small group of advanced technology industries, and most notably on the aircraft industry, and with very uncertain results in terms of production and profitable sales. Not only has the rest of the economy been burdened with the costs of financing through taxation these expensive efforts to promote selected industries, but it has been argued that it has been denuded of scarce scientific and technical manpower which could have been put to better use if left to find its way into those industries that could make profitable use of it.

The supply of labour has a complex relationship with the growth of an economy and attention has frequently been drawn to the slow growth of the working population in Britain as a possible cause of our slow growth relatively to continental countries. In 1966 a plausible but partial economic theory influenced Government to try to promote growth via increasing the supply of labour to manufacturing industry. Professor Kaldor's theory on which the Selective Employment Tax was based was an interesting attempt to account for the faster growth rates in some other countries but did not provide an adequate theoretical basis for his prescription of using discriminatory taxation to redistribute labour from services to manufacturing in Britain. While there may have been other arguments for this particular tax at the time (including the fact that services escaped other taxes that were levied on manufacturing, and the need for some new source of tax revenue), it was extremely anomalous as a policy for growth because it ignored the contribution to growth of service industries, and the need for many manufacturing industries to reduce their labour force by raising productivity rather than to increase it. The most serious problem, however, common to all these policies operating on the supply side, was how to ensure that the resources induced into industry by means of the various incentives could be profitably used.

Attempts had been made to solve this problem by action to raise expectations of the future level of demand. The theory rested on one of the (optional) interpretations of the meaning of the residual term in models of economic growth. Up to half the observed growth in some continental countries in the 1950s and early 1960s was unexplained by increased inputs of capital and labour. If this growth could be explained as being brought about by expectations of future demand in those countries, that is, by the willingness of business to expand because of buoyant expectations of future sales, then it could support a prescription of direct operation on the expectations of firms in order to persuade them to increase their investment, research, labour, and hence output.

In France, a theory stressing the role of demand and the possibility of increasing it via planning methods not entirely dissimilar from those used in the socialist planned economies, probably made some contribution to the growth of the economy in the 1950s. But economic theory had little to do with the evolution of this policy; the theory followed and explained the policy rather than initiated it. Moreover, this method was successful in France only under rather special conditions, which could not be assumed either for other countries or for France in other periods. Thus in the later evolution of French policy, indicative planning became of less significance to growth performance.

Attempts to apply an expansionist strategy for increasing growth, coupled with planning methods closely modelled on the French experience, to the British economy in the 1960s, in the National Economic Development Council with associated Economic Development Committees and the National Plan, foundered because the special conditions in which such methods could contribute to growth did not exist in the UK at that time. The result has been, in Britain at least, the discrediting, at least for some years, of attempts at medium-term planning. While the causes of this particular episode in the history of economic policy are certainly at least as much political as economic, economics did not come well out of it.

During the 1960s when these various 'experiments' were being made in influencing growth via the supply-side factors: investment, R and D, and labour, and via demand expectations, much attention had been given also to the role of external payments problems in slowing down growth. For many years it was held that the exchange rate was over-valued and that periodic restrictive measures intended to correct the chronic payments deficits disrupted industry's investment plans and dashed the expectations of demand that governments were at the same time trying to raise by other means. Devaluation was finally used in 1967, and in 1972–3 the Government made a renewed attempt at the expansionist strategy for achieving faster growth, this time with a (downward) floating exchange rate. While based on economic advice, the policy could not be based on any firm calculations as to its effects; it could only be regarded as a deliberate taking of considerable risks in a situation where the consequences of not making an attempt at faster growth looked about as bad as those of failing in the attempt. Since much depended on the response and restraint of the social partners preventing the exchange rate from falling to an unacceptably low level, the success or otherwise of this policy appeared to rest at least as much on sociological factors as on economic calculation.

Finally, we may mention another method of promoting growth that came into vogue especially following the failure of the National Plan in the mid-1960s. This is a micro-economic rather than macro-economic policy, the deliberate restructuring of industry, and more specifically increasing the size of firms, with the intention of creating more efficient units. Economic theory does not have much to do directly with this prescription, though various elements of micro-economics, such as the study of the effects of scale on the unit costs of firms, are relevant. The policy is, rather, determined by the failure of policies based on other economic theories to have the desired effects, and by these failures being attributed to the structure of capitalist industry. Larger firms, it is argued, will have closer relations with government, which will make it easier for government to influence their investment, export, etc. policies. At its extreme this argument calls for the nationalisation of industry in order to make government control fully effective. This policy has been implemented in part by subsidies given selectively to promote the growth of some firms (especially in advanced technology) and to ensure the survival of others (especially those faced with foreign competition, and those whose demise would cause large redundancies). There may be all kinds of arguments in favour of restructuring industry and of change in the relations between industry and government, but it certainly seems to have little chance of promoting economic growth if it continues to lead to subsidies to inefficient firms at the expense of profitable firms since this represents a reallocation of resources in an inefficient direction. Its most serious effect is probably most difficult to measure: that it leads to a situation in which firms, and especially large firms, come to the conclusion that the Government will always come to their rescue. Perhaps allowing 'lame ducks' to go under is socially unacceptable

and should not be contemplated by any government. But if this is
so, we must find some other way of promoting economic growth, for
it certainly is not promoted by subsidising firms, even to the extent
of over 50 per cent of their costs of production, as happened in the
case of some large shipbuilders.

I now turn to consider areas of economic theory not so directly
related to economic growth policy, but whose relevance to the
growth of the economy is considerable.

Growth and the theory of resource allocation

Failure to understand clearly the causes of economic growth has also
tended to undermine the value of economics in areas where it
appeared more firmly established. If the causes of growth are not
understood, then it is impossible to assert the primacy of a theoretical system that emphasises the optimum allocation of given
resources; for it is impossible to say whether the effects of operating
an economy in accordance with the optimum (static) allocation of
resources increases or reduces the growth rate. If the growth rate
should be reduced the loss of welfare resulting from slower growth
could be greater than the gain in welfare deriving from the optimum
allocation of existing resources.

The theory of the allocation of resources via the prices of goods
and factors was the most intensively developed body of economic
thought down to the 1930s. This micro-economic theory had most
influence on the thought and actions of economic agents, and the
basic economic hypotheses developed in this area continue to be the
most generally recognised contribution of economics to human
knowledge. In recent years the employment of economists to give
detailed advice on pricing and investment decisions has become
usual at both enterprise and government level, and more and more
managers have studied economics either formally or informally.
This dissemination of the rather simple principles of economic
allocation has produced innumerable benefits throughout the
economy, which must certainly in aggregate cover the costs of
employing academic, business and government economists, and
probably provide in addition a very high rate of return on the social
investment in their training. Especially in the problems susceptible
to cost-benefit analysis economists have shown constructive imagination in applying basic concepts in areas where they have previously been ignored. Progress in widening the scope of resource
allocation theory has been one of the achievements of recent years,
despite the controversy that inevitably surrounds the conclusions

of major cost-benefit analyses. Achieving the correct pricing policy and investment decisions in a British nationalised industry, or in a large private company is of undoubted importance to human welfare. Achieving the most efficient overall national allocation can also yield great benefits.

Nevertheless, there has been great dissatisfaction with the economic theory of resource allocation, for two main reasons which may be termed technical and social. The technical problem has been that, in the pursuit of simplicity and clarity of theoretical exposition, economists have abstracted excessively from the world whose behaviour they were trying to explain and predict. Substantial modifications of micro-economic theory in the 1930s and after, useful though they have been, represented a belated attempt to come to terms with the world as it is, and a not too successful one. For the new models of modified competition are still over-simplified, and it has become apparent that economists fail to incorporate into their theory essential aspects of the administrative structures underlying enterprise and government decisions. Economic theory may explain why the production of a single commodity should be increased or decreased marginally at a particular moment, but it has still relatively little to tell us about why firms should choose to produce a particular range of commodities, why they should or should not grow, etc.

The social problem about the theory of resource allocation has been its influence in creating and maintaining a set of values that has become increasingly unacceptable. Aware of this criticism, economists have adopted what in the modern political jargon is called a 'low profile', trying to distinguish the positive from the normative and defining their role as that of technicians, giving advice only on the positive questions. This self-denial is a desirable expression of the modesty proper to a science that wishes to avoid having excessive pretensions deflated, but the position is not easily tenable. The most technical economic discussion is laden with value problems, and more important, the starting point and the whole method of the economics of resource allocation is a particular set of values. Whether he likes it or not, the economist is a social manipulator. While the separation of technical economic from social economic issues continues to be essential, the familiar criticism that there is no value-free social science is unanswerable.

What I have called the technical and the social problems of the basic economic theory of resource allocation both create immense difficulties for economic growth and some of these implications are mentioned later.

Growth and the distribution of income

Economists have always been uneasy about the place of the distribution of income in their models. In marginalist theory it follows
from the rewards and incentives required for the efficient allocation
of resources. Difficulty arises in reconciling this economic explanation with the powerful social influences on income distribution.
Economists have usually solved the problem by asserting that social
forces cannot operate regardless of the limits set by economic forces,
and that economic variables themselves incorporate many of the
social variables affecting income distribution.

Even if the economic theory of distribution did hold good as an
explanation of why people receive the incomes they do, it would
not constitute any case, either on equity or efficiency grounds, for
accepting the distribution that arises.

That there is no reason in equity to accept an income distribution
which arises out of the system of economic incentives has long been
recognised politically, and a solution to the problem has been
attempted through the redistribution of income by progressive taxation and social security benefits. But since gross incomes adjust
through the pricing system to compensate for taxes, all that a redistri-
butory system could hope to achieve in the long term was to create
a gap between gross incomes that had already adjusted to tax, and
so-called net-of-tax incomes. The redistribution between gross and
net income is meaningful only in the short term and as accountants'
shorthand; it has little economic significance.

Failure to solve the problem of equity arising out of the way
incomes are determined in a social system that emphasises efficient
allocation has been compounded by the failure of this system to
allocate efficiently the most important resource, labour. Social
constraints apart, inequalities in the distribution of income, while
they may have improved the static distribution of a given labour
force at a given moment of time, have, through the distortions of
educational opportunity, adversely affected the quality of the labour
force over time. Through their effects on social cohesion they have
also affected attitudes in ways adverse to the reduction of industrial
strife and to the self-restraint in economic behaviour that has always
been an important variable, but underestimated by economists in
favour of their maximising economic man whose behaviour is easier
to predict. The relevance of these rather dogmatic comments may be
briefly supported by reference to the social problems which are
commonly recognised as important determinants of the current
growth prospects of the British economy. Resentment at the price of

land and houses, concern about 'insider' deals, the militant mood of some trade unions, are reflections not simply of inflation, but of inflation exacerbating inequalities of income, wealth and opportunity. These are, of course, political more than economic issues. The question for economists is how to make their theories relevant to them.

Growth and the control of fluctuations

The control of unemployment has been among the greatest recent successes of economics. Since the Second World War fluctuations in activity have never reached the proportions of the 1930s, or even of the nineteenth century. New policies on the part of governments apparently were important in this improvement, and economic theory certainly played an important role in forming the new policies. But confidence in the value of the new macro-economics, well nigh universal in the 1940s and 1950s began to be eroded in the 1960s. There are numerous reasons why this happened, some of them no reflection on economics as such. Governments and electorates as we have mentioned before have become more ambitious in their requirements and often demand the impossible. Institutions and behaviour have changed in ways that destroyed or radically altered functional relationships on which economic theories and successful policies had been based, and the necessary modification of theories is not easy because of inevitable lags in the provision and analysis of statistical data describing the new structure of economic forces. The recent disrepute of the Phillips Curve is probably the widest known example of this phenomenon, though there are many others, especially in the monetary field.

Other deficiencies of macro-economics are intrinsic to the science. First, the technical weakness of micro-economics, referred to above, has not only represented an annoying void in itself, but has undermined progress in macro-economics. If economists could not produce satisfactory explanations of how businessmen behaved, the value of their advice to governments on the use of macro-economic policy instruments was reduced, since these had to operate through the decisions of businessmen. Many policies, from investment allowances to bank rate and selective employment tax, have remained of uncertain effectiveness on account of the ignorance about the way business would react to them. Assessments of the micro-economic effects of demand management policies, carried out by some who had been closely involved in practising them, produced rather negative results. Far from confirming the earlier assumption that economic analysis had contributed to the success of policy, it seemed that, if anything, policy had been ill-timed, and thus worsened rather than improved an economic performance which in regard to stability, happened for other reasons to be better than in the 1920s and 1930s. Though many of the lags in deciding and implementing a change of economic policy may be considered to lie outside the sphere of economics, economists may have been at fault in advising policies without taking adequate account of these problems of timing.

While apparent success in controlling unemployment was never matched in respect of inflation, only in recent years has the acceleration of inflation revealed the full extent of the weakness of macro-economics. Changing institutional structures, especially the growth of multi-national industrial and banking enterprises, have played a large part in undermining confidence in economists' ability to understand and to help control the macro-economy. But weaknesses in the basic economic models, and especially their failure to allow adequately for administrative, structural and social factors, have also been evident.

Growth and international resource allocation

The extension of the domestic theory of resource allocation to the international economy is both elegant and powerful, and international economics has been one of the most prestigious and glamorous parts of economic theory. Under the influence of international economists world trade was progressively liberalised in the 1950s and 1960s by the removal of quotas and reduction of tariffs.

While trade showed enormous increases, measures of the welfare gains brought about by this liberalisation indicated that it may have been unimportant beside the other causes of growth in output per head. Some of the fastest growth rates were enjoyed in countries which did not play a large part in world trade, while growth in some countries has been adversely affected by problems arising out of dependence on trade.

Inconvenient arguments for protection survived economists' scathing and comprehensive condemnation. In particular, the small gains from liberal trading policies appeared irrelevant when set beside the loss of output from unemployed resources, especially of labour, that might be brought back into use by protectionist policies. The old mercantilist position remained enshrined in the infant-industry case for protection, an argument that economists could do little to counter except to assert that governments would not know when the infant had grown up. But since trade theory is largely limited to static hypotheses, economists had no better claim than politicians to know when the infant industry no longer needed protection. This is another example of the limitations of a science that does not have much to say about economic growth and the long term.

As if this was not bad enough, while economists and governments were chipping away at the most overt forms of interference with the international allocation of resources, the economic reality with which they were trying to cope was changing so rapidly that their efforts appeared increasingly irrelevant. The growth of the significance in trade of the multinational corporation blurred the distinction between national and international economics on which governments were, and still are, in large part, operating. A new international theory of the firm is therefore required to explain in a systematic way the behaviour of these new institutions. The spread of non-tariff barriers meant that before the tariffs had been removed, they had been replaced, and more than replaced, by a set of barriers to international trade that were not amenable to anything like the relatively simple inter-governmental negotiation of reciprocal reductions that will do for tariffs. The proliferating industrial and regional subsidies, public procurement preferences and technical barriers have created a wide plane of interaction between domestic policies and external commercial policy. The maintenance of an efficient international allocation of resources therefore requires a far more complex reconciliation with the objectives of domestic economic policies. Economists are beginning to turn their attention to this problem, but so little research has been done that they have little constructive advice to offer in this extremely important policy area. Simultaneously with these immense changes the international monetary adjustment system broke down; in part on account of the financial freedom achieved by the multinationals.

While many of the problems for economic science derived therefore from the rapid changes in the world economic structure, a fundamental weakness had been apparent in the economic model all along: namely, that an international system based largely on national self-interest and competitive behaviour still depended on the exercise of some self-restraint for its stability in the same way that, as mentioned earlier, domestic economic systems based on individual self-interest and competitive behaviour require nevertheless considerable self-restraint on the part of the social partners. The institutional reinstatement of self-restraint in international economic behaviour has little to do with short-term maximisation by individual firms or governments, so the solution to this problem does not lie within the scope of existing economic analysis.

D

Growth and regional economics

For political, social and other reasons there has been at least as much interest in regional balance as in growth of the UK economy as a whole, and economics has been called on to assist the development of regional policy by analysing the causes of regional economic problems, especially unemployment. The study of the micro-economic structure of the regions attempts to answer the question what kind of industry could be successfully relocated. The study of the macro-economic structure leads to advice on the influence that general macro-economic incentives and injections of spending could have. Economists have also attempted to answer the question how far regional policies contribute to or detract from national economic growth. The apparently successful application of economic science to regional problems appears to compensate for some of the deficiencies in applying it to overall management of the economy and to international trade. If it is impossible to run the economy at a sufficiently high level of demand to eliminate unemployment because the unemployment is concentrated in certain areas on account of the geographical immobility of labour, then regional policy to create a better balance in industrial development relatively to the distribution of the population seeking work appears a sensible solution. Similarly, if the desired participation in the international division of labour is rejected because of the waste involved in (regionally concentrated) unemployment created by import competition, regional policy appears to resolve the dilemma.

However, far too many loose ends are involved in these justifications of regional policy for economists to feel secure that they have made a contribution. In relation to domestic economic management, doubt must remain whether the new regional analysis is reconcilable with the efficient allocation of resources in the long term. Until the millennium arrives and economists are capable of carrying out the massive long-term cost-benefit analyses of regional policy necessary to determine what is the efficient long-term regional structure of the economy, they cannot be sure that the gains from reducing unemployment have not been secured at the cost of a permanent reduction in national productivity. In relation to international trade, it is similarly impossible to be sure that the adjustment to import competition involved in a successful regional policy is not bought at excessive cost in terms of the loss of the gains from international specialisation.

Conclusions

Why is it that economic science appears of such limited relevance to the growth performance in a period of unprecedented expansion in terms of numbers of economists and scope of their employment? The foregoing brief comments on a number of areas where economic theory ought to help the formation of policies that will increase economic growth suggest that the reasons are both exogenous and endogenous to the discipline. Economics has certainly faced great difficulties arising out of the rapid changes in the phenomena it is trying to understand and predict. It has also come under immense pressures from governments and others who insist on answers to currently unanswerable questions. But the profession has not reacted well to these outside forces, and some of the difficulties may be of economists' own creation.

Economists are perhaps excessively absorbed in the narcissistic contemplation of the beauties of their 200-year-old science. They enjoy building simple and elegant models, which have great aesthetic appeal. But if the attempt to build them involves excessively unrealistic hypotheses, then the practical value of the science is sacrificed to its aesthetics just as surely as in the creation of ancient myths.

It is difficult to refuse the many requests for enlightenment from those who have not been admitted to the sacred mysteries, to refuse to answer questions, even if one knows the answer is unknown, and all too easy to persuade oneself of the correctness of the reply that springs facilely to mind in these circumstances. The fact that every other economist will have his own, different, answer in such situations, far from undermining the arrogance reinforces it, for controversies in the Journals are always good fun and enhance professional reputation; while if the outsiders are mystified, so much the better for the external reputation of the profession.

It may be objected that in having a go at providing answers to unanswerable questions economists are not only responding properly to the urgent requests of their fellow humans for enlightenment, but are indeed following proper scientific methods. The proposition of hypothesis and counter-hypothesis is well established in natural science. However, there is a difference between proposing a theory of the universe, and explaining the causes of economic growth in the United Kingdom. If the natural scientist is wrong, little harm will have been done, but given the influence of social scientists on governments desperate for a policy, if they are wrong it is very possible that harm may be done. Of course, governments will persist in asking for advice from economists, even if they are wrong; partly because it will not be easy to *prove* they are wrong; partly because governments must have an economic policy, no policy being a policy that many would agree is very wrong indeed. But since the internecine warfare within the profession shows that most economists are wrong most of the time, the first quality any economist needs is modesty.

The solutions to the dilemmas economists find themselves in cannot be simple, or they would have been proposed long ago. But then we are all so busy practising economics that it is not easy to find time for appraisal of what we are doing. This deficiency is probably the responsibility of academic rather than official economists, since the former have more time to stand back from current pressures and think deeply about their subject. On the other hand, official and business economists must have a more vivid awareness of the limitations of economics in practical situations.

Research in economics needs to be more continuously aware of the fundamental scientific problems, and above all of the contributions of other disciplines to all the problems we like to think of as primarily economic. Economists must be more ready to write so as to be understood by others, and more ready to promote active co-operation with other disciplines. A sense of superiority of economics among the social sciences certainly appears misplaced. We must avoid the over-simplification that comes from using a crude economic variable to stand for complex social forces outside our comprehension.

Above all, in the presentation of advice economists should make clear their own doubts rather than try to win arguments by a rhetoric that glosses over the uncertainties. If this results in economic policy becoming less ambitious, we shall only be in the same position as the engineers who take immense pains to ensure that their bridges and aeroplanes do not fall down.

Technology and the Quality of Life

*Graham Bannock**

1

It seems to me that several generally-accepted views about the rate
of technological change and its role in economic growth are not easily
substantiated. Most economists have also, until relatively recently at
least, been remarkably silent upon the whole question of the quality
of life. This, to the layman seems odd, since it is the quality of life
(which ultimately means the satisfaction we obtain from it), which is
the end result of all the material endeavours about which economics
deals as a subject. The reason for the neglect of quality by economists is, of course, that it cannot be satisfactorily measured.

For a long time economists have side-stepped this capital difficulty
by working in terms of ordinal utility—that is to say it is assumed
that the consumer cannot measure his own satisfaction with any
particular good or combination of goods but he is able to rank
quantities of goods on the basis of preference or indifference. In this
way, the economist is able to infer that the consumer obtains *more*
satisfaction from one combination of goods and services than
others, although he cannot measure the absolute amount of that
satisfaction. It follows from this, and telescoping the chain of
argument somewhat, that where the pricing of goods in the market
reflects consumer selection of these parcels of goods and services
that give maximum utility the valuation of all goods in the national
product provides an index of consumer satisfaction although not, of
course, an absolute measure of that satisfaction. Subject to one
important qualification it would be generally true to say, I think,
that most economists would agree that roughly speaking (and
ignoring changes in the distribution of income) a UK national income
of £50 billion reflects a higher level of UK consumer satisfaction
than one of £40 billion.

* Partner, Economists Advisory Group.

The important qualification is, of course, that only private costs and benefits are allowed for in the national income and that social costs and benefits—that is to say those that are borne or conferred indiscriminately by society by the processes of production or consumption—are not. This is one important point at which economics has long recognised the effects of technology upon the quality of life. It recognises that atmospheric pollution, for example, gives dissatisfaction and therefore generates a negative satisfaction by which national income ought to be adjusted. The difficulty is that since consumers do not express their dissatisfaction through the price mechanism, for example, by buying goods with or without the pollution that their production or consumption creates, we have no quantities by which we can actually adjust the national income data as an index of consumer satisfaction.

But our indicators of national income and output are subject to many more qualifications. There has, for example, been argument about the effects on GNP of the exclusion of unpaid housework by housewives but there is a much more important qualification which has received little attention and which is very relevant to my subject today. The valuation of goods and services in the GNP at market prices only has meaning under conditions of perfect competition with its assumptions about perfect knowledge and freedom of choice. The theory of consumer demand which underpins our use of national income and output statistics as indicators of satisfaction does not allow for the possibility that the consumer does not have freedom of choice or that his choice can be influenced by the suppliers.[1] If the Government insists on providing me with a service that I do not want such as the services of a tax inspector, the GNP still reflects that person's economic output. Similarly, if a soap company employs a beautiful young woman to persuade my wife to use a face lotion that she does not really want or the local garage presents my small son with a plastic gold sovereign that he does not really want, then GNP reflects their services and the manufacturing activity involved. Since at least half of economic output is now, to a greater or lesser extent, affected in this way in advanced countries we have to be increasingly sceptical of the utility of national income statistics as indicators of economic welfare.

Now I believe that it is no exaggeration to say that these measurement problems and the real problems of economic organisation that underlie them are now so acute that we are now at risk of becoming adrift on the sea of economic and technological change without charts or compass. We are also at risk of becoming rudderless since the price mechanism can no longer necessarily point us in the direction in which we want to go—the direction of more satisfaction. This price mechanism is not, as I have suggested, functioning, or it is functioning only very imperfectly so that our economic system is rigidly set in producing, not only the wrong goods, but producing them in ways that are creating strong negative satisfactions. This is why the Government considers itself justified to intervene more and more in setting standards of quality, in regulating pollution, in arbitrating between private and social costs and benefits and in many other ways. But it seems to be a losing battle since this intervention inevitably rigidifies the system still further. New problems arise faster than the old ones are solved because intervention from above treats symptoms rather than causes.

2

A common, but I believe totally mistaken belief, is that these problems are all the fault of technology; that our ability to find new ways of doing things outstrips our ability to harness technology to enhance satisfaction rather than impair it.

A little reflection will soon produce an alarming list of contemporary problems which are popularly attributed to the use of modern technology and technological change. In compiling such a list I have restricted it broadly to the products of the revolution which began in the 1750s in agricultural and engineering technology. The technological revolution in medicine came later than those in agriculture and the then so-called mechanical arts and its benefits are, so far, little questioned.[2]

Here, without of course, accepting all of it as the sole or even principal result of technological change, is my list:

Environment: ugly or monotonous new buildings, destruction of old buildings; noise, soil, air and water pollution; soil erosion; destruction of scenery and natural life, risks of disaster through explosion, radiation, etc.

Economic disruption: vulnerability of services supplied by large plants to breakdown, sabotage and strikes; depletion of natural resources; lack of flexibility in response to changes in tastes or needs.

Social disruption: alienation of workforce by eliminating jobs or job satisfaction; destruction of communities; urbanisation and congestion; spread of bureaucracy and regimentation; premature retirement; pace and strain.

Quality and choice: processed foods inferior to traditional foods; goods less durable, more difficult to repair; planned obsolescence; diminished choice.

This is not a complete list (you will notice for example that I have omitted the effects of military technology), nor perhaps are its sub-classifications entirely satisfactory but it provides a rough summary of the evils put down to modern technology. It is a depressing list and is certainly much longer and more complicated than a list of the generally perceived benefits of technology. These might be summarised as:

> Greater abundance of the necessities and many 'luxuries' of life including food, shelter, clothing, heat and light, education, books and entertainment.
> Increased personal mobility and vastly improved communications.
> Reduced physical effort and discomfort.

This is certainly a short and simple list and it could be endlessly expanded by specifying, in detail, the material benefits which technology has brought us. You might think that I have rather loaded the comparison against technology but I am not attempting here to balance the benefits of technology against its costs. I am rather trying to discuss the nature of the benefits and costs, the way we select them and the extent to which they are interconnected. Just reading out this list and comparing it with the previous list brings out the important point I want to make, however, and that is that the benefits of technology seem mainly to be *quantitative* in nature while the associated disadvantages have been *qualitative*. In this sense modern technology has clearly had an adverse effect upon many aspects of the quality of life. The question I want to try and answer is, is this inevitable?

3

I define technology as the application of systematic knowledge to human work. It is not, in practice, an unambiguous term. For example although the central meaning of the term has to do with the use of tools and artifacts it does sometimes depend upon other disciplines such as scientific knowledge and methods of organisation. Technology is not merely applied science because it often runs ahead of science—we do things without always knowing exactly how or why we do them except that they are effective. Early technology—craft skill—was almost entirely of this sort. One of the most distinctive features of modern technology, I think, is that it is increasingly science-based and to those qualified to receive it, easily communicable by demonstration and printed material rather than acquired skill.

The generally-held view about technology, and the one that lays at its door all the problems I have listed, appears to be based upon two assumptions:[3]

(i) That technological development in general is analogous to the pursuit of knowledge in the pure sciences and that because of this the progress of technological knowledge is an inevitable and an autonomous factor in economic development.

(ii) That technological change is accelerating for well-known reasons, that this is the main source of difficulty in our society and that the present course of technological development can only be interrupted at the expense of economic growth.

Neither of these assumptions can be supported, I think, and together they distract us from the solutions to the problems we face. The first is hardly ever stated explicitly but it lurks behind such familiar phrases as 'technological necessity', 'the requirements of high technology', 'technology has a momentum of its own'. The impression given by these phrases is that our search for better ways of doing things is independent of the organisation of production: that technology is an absolute truth to be sought for its own sake and then to be used regardless of the outcome, that how something is done is independent of the people doing it or their reasons for wanting to. Expressed bluntly in this way the idea is obviously absurd, but so too is the statement that technology itself is a problem for society. Technology is nothing more than the way we choose to solve the problems of work: if any given technological solution creates more problems than it solves, then there is no reason to apply it. It is no good blaming the hammer if you drop it on your toe. The difference between the pursuit of knowledge in pure science and technology in this respect is that in the former we are trying to gain an understanding of the external world while in the latter we are trying to solve man-made problems, often using the results of science but always within the framework of man-made constraints. Problems with technology arise, I believe, because we have chosen to work within the wrong constraints or an insufficient number of constraints.

This brings me to the second conventional assumption about technology which is that we can only alter the present course of technological development at the expense of economic growth. This

raises much more difficult issues and is the main point with which
I want to deal in this paper. But first I should like to suggest to you
that thought on this subject is very much clouded by the cliché
about accelerating technological change as a source of difficulty in
society.

It is asserted frequently that technological change is accelerating.
Evidence marshalled in support of this assertion includes the rapid
diminution in the time taken to develop and introduce certain
inventions: radio took so long, television so much less, colour
television so much less again. This is a measurement of output but
it is not at all clear what the units of this measurement are. Is
television an equivalent element of technological change to the
wireless, was the invention of the transistor more or less important
than that of penicillin? These questions need to be answered before
we can draw inferences about the rate of change. To an economist
it would be necessary to attach weights to these elements in technological change before meaningful comparisons could be made and
even then the difficulty of allowing for the interdependence of such
inventions as television and colour television would have to be dealt
with. This has not, to my knowledge, been done. The rest of the
evidence for accelerating technological change is based upon
measures of input such as the numbers of qualified scientists and
engineers at work or expenditure on research and development. Now
whilst input may be a fairly reliable indicator of outputs in the
short term for manufacturing industry, e.g. y tons of iron-ore produce x tons of pig iron, it is of little help in estimating the output of
such an unpredictable thing as technological innovation or any other
activity involving human imagination and creativity. My own
opinion, for what it is worth, is that historically technological
change has occurred in bursts but that there is no satisfactory evidence for any acceleration in, say, this century so far.

Society is also, according to such writers as Alvin Toffler,[4] in a
state of shock following this accelerating rate of change. I think
that you could argue the contrary. Technological change, defined
as the means of applying systematic knowledge to human work is
not changing anything like rapidly enough. To take two examples
from communications that spring to mind. I travel to work on an
inefficient underground system that was laid down not long after
the turn of the century. I also have trouble with the telephone. Yet
the know-how exists to overcome both these problems: systematic
knowledge is *not* being applied because of shortage of capital or
political will or other reasons. In these cases my difficulties arise not
from an excess of technological change but from an insufficiency of
it.

4

What is the general course of technological change then and why is it generally assumed that we cannot alter it except at the expense of economic growth?

There are, of course, many distinctive trends in modern technology. To give a few examples from manufacturing industry: there is a general trend towards the use of lighter and natural materials; there is more moulding and forming and less fabrication: both these things lead to fewer finishing processes; batch processes are giving way to continuous processes; operating speeds of all types of machinery are going up and there is an increasing use of electronic control gear. Production is generally becoming more capital- and less labour-intensive and there has been a general trend towards a redesign of products to make them easier and cheaper to produce. It would be generally accepted however, I think, that the most striking trend in modern technology has been that towards an increased scale of activity. Giant chemical plants and buildings, enormous tankers and aircraft, large factories employing thousands of workers; these are things the layman thinks of as characteristic of modern technology.

It will also often be these things that he thinks of if you ask him to consider the disadvantages of technology. In fact some, though by no means all, of these disadvantages are the direct or indirect result of scale. Many of them are not primarily the result of scale, it should be emphasised—a thousand small chimneys may well create more pollution nuisance than one large one. But it is upon the problems of scale that I should like to concentrate because I think that they are the most important, and the most misunderstood.

My argument is that the adoption of smaller-scale technology could contribute enormously to the quality of life and is, therefore, directed at the solution of those problems that can be wholly or partly attributable to great scale—the visual intrusion of large plants, the alienation of the workforce, the inferior quality of mass-produced food, for example. Ultimately this argument reduces to a plea for more individual human control over the quality of output which I think is vastly easier when that output is produced in smaller units. This is because in a smaller unit both the consumer and the workpeople can have more influence over the nature of the product and the way it is produced. I suspect that the argument does not apply at all comprehensively to some types of production, for example, oil production. To admit this does not affect the argument which still applies to other industries. Perhaps too we should be trying to avoid the use of products which can only be produced on a small scale in favour of those that can. Windmills instead of power stations, for example.

The reason why we cannot alter the course of development towards greater scale except at the expense of economic growth is, of course, generally thought to be obvious: it is because this would mean raising real costs by sacrificing the economies of scale. Now I question this argument for a number of reasons.

First, although undoubtedly production costs do fall as the scale of many processes increases there are limits to this (at least with present knowledge). The decline in unit costs typically falls sharply at first and then levels off. It is not too difficult to document this for particular processes but it is very difficult indeed to do so for the complex groups of complementary processes which are typical of modern industry because different processes tend to have different optimum scales of production and because there are diseconomies of scale in co-ordination that seem to set in rather early. Certainly there is ample evidence that overall incremental production economies of scale from further growth would be very small indeed in most large-scale industries today and that the economies obtained in many large projects are easily offset by other factors. It has been calculated, for example, that the internal rate of return (DCF) for a 1,000-ton-per-day ammonia plant is 26 per cent if the plant achieves 100 per cent capacity utilisation from year one and is completed on schedule in two years. If, however, the plant is delayed one year the rate of return falls to 21 per cent and if full capacity utilisation is not achieved until the third year of operation then the rate of return falls to 13 per cent.[5] This is a difficult subject which I have attempted to deal with more fully elsewhere.[6] It is not essential to my argument and I simply ask you to share my suspicions that theoretical economies which are so difficult to document in the event are unlikely to be vitally important.

Second, even if there is considerable 'economic' benefit to be gained from large-scale technology how do we know that this benefit is not offset by the extra GNP social and private costs that I mentioned earlier and which are not reflected in our measures of economic growth? Clearly we do not know because we have no measure of them but I doubt very much if they are offset. If this were so, then at some point in time large-scale technology may have begun to have a net negative effect upon human welfare. For example, large-scale brewing requires centralisation of national production in a small number of plants. Increased transport costs compared with smaller, local, breweries wipe out a significant proportion of the economies gained. Moreover, the longer chain of distribution and large-scale technology rule out the traditional brewing process and the substitution of keg for cask beer which has a longer 'shelf life' and is more easily brewed on a large scale. Heavy marketing expenditure is then necessary to persuade the customer to drink keg instead of his traditional draught bitter. How can we calculate the net effect upon consumer satisfaction?

Third, and equally important, how do we *know* that economic growth could not proceed at the same speed or even faster with smaller-scale technology? Again, we do not know because there has hitherto been no strong incentive for society to pursue small-scale technology. The constraints upon technological development have been primarily private (as opposed to social) cost constraints and managerial constraints. At the same time, for reasons which have had more to do with taxation, government policies and the workings of the capital market than technology, the organisation of business has increasingly been concentrated into larger units. Large units of organisation have little incentive to develop small-scale technology and many good reasons for pursuing large-scale technology.[7] For these reasons, therefore, the vast majority of society's capital resources have been devoted to large-scale technology. In short, I am suggesting to you that technology is not independent of social organisation as it is generally supposed but, on the contrary, is very dependent upon it.

I should like to underline this point because it is very important. If technology were like pure science, simply a seeking after some absolute truth, it *could* be regarded as an uncontrollable force in economic development. But it is not an uncontrollable force, indeed by definition technology is not a force at all but simply the means by which men carry out the work they choose to do. If they wish to choose something different or choose to do it in a different way they are free to do so. To argue that any set of choices other than the ones we are making now would involve a sacrifice is to assume that technology cannot be adapted to produce better results by other means. This is very unlikely: the whole history of technology is that man has always found a way to do the things he really wants to do in the material world. There is no reason to suppose that he cannot continue to do so,

I had better make it clear that I am not expecting that the development of smaller-scale technology would necessarily lead to greater technical efficiency at plant level because it was small but rather indirectly because it would allow organisational and other changes that would increase overall economic efficiency. I shall give an example of an instance where this has been done in a moment.

It follows from all this, I think, that our problems do not lie in the nature of technology but in our social, political and economic institutions: it is these that are at fault, not technology. The present tendency in these institutions (companies, central and local government and organised labour and other interest groups) is towards centralisation, inflexibility and greater scale. Technology is reflecting this tendency towards concentration and will presumably continue to do so while it persists.

5

I would not pretend to forecast precisely how technology could develop to permit a smaller, more human and less environmentally damaging scale of economic activity. There are many possibilities. In the service and knowledge industries real-time computer systems, video-telephone and conference television systems should permit the dispersal of employment. The trend away from the use of heavy materials such as cast iron in consumer goods and towards lighter materials has greatly reduced the necessity for the massive satanic mills of the past. I am optimistic too that many of our present problems will encourage the dispersal of economic activity into smaller units and environmental improvement. Strong forces are now at work. The rising cost of energy and many basic raw materials will discourage the massive production of throw-away packaging.

The rising cost of energy should help swing the balance away from centralised, national sources of production back towards local sources of supply. This could have a favourable effect upon the quality of output as in the bread and beer industries for example. I find it cheering to reflect that even the tax system, through discouraging the purchase of certain goods and services with after-tax income when the taxpayer can provide them for himself at a lower after-tax cost, will continue to stimulate the development of small-scale technology!

A good recent example of the way technology can allow us to turn a seemingly immutable trend through 180 degrees, if there is an incentive to do so, can be found in the motor industry. You may have read of Volvo's successful experiment in abandoning the assembly line in car production. Volvo is incidentally, as car manufacturers go, a small firm. What they have done is to design and build a factory in which small groups of workers assemble a complete car in static bays, using advanced equipment instead of stationing the men at points on a moving belt so that they may carry out repetitive operations as the belt moves. I understand that although this procedure increases stock and capital costs it does not slow output and greatly increases quality and job satisfaction with a corresponding reduction in labour difficulties and absenteeism.

This experiment is now being studied by several other motor manufacturers. It is significant because it shows what can be done when completely fresh thinking is used to break out of a very long-established technological process. If you think about it, it also raises many questions about the real reasons for the success of the assembly line system. It now seems quite possible that the assembly line itself had little or nothing to do with the increased output which followed its introduction. This increase may have been the result of the redesign of the product that became necessary for flow production, improved stock flow and control processes and other factors. The incentive to experiment with the abandonment of the assembly line was chronically deteriorating labour relations and quality problems and therefore precisely analogous to the extra-GNP elements that I discussed earlier. In this case the constraints and incentives were strong enough to stimulate an attempt at a new approach.

My conclusion is that if we are to exploit the potential of technology to enhance the quality of life these extra-GNP elements have to be brought to bear more fully upon the workings of the economic system by means of appropriate constraints and incentives. This will require the solution of the social and political problems of economic organisation: if we can do that, previous experience suggests that the technological problems will look after themselves. If we can scrap such a well entrenched symbol of technological inevitability as the assembly line what could we not do if our whole economic system could be made more sensitive and responsive to human needs?

Notes

1. See J. K. Galbraith, *The New Industrial State*, Hamish Hamilton, 1967.
2. The side effects of certain drugs, test-tube babies and the care of the very old or infirm are the subject of contemporary criticism, many others are looming for the future.
3. I am referring to lay opinion here; the autonomy of technological development is a matter for dispute among economists. See *Science, Invention & Economic Growth*, N. Rosenberg, The Economic Journal March 1974; nor do all economists accept the view that technological change is accelerating, see, *The Sources of Invention*, Jewkes, Sawers & Stillerman, Macmillan, 1969.
4. Alvin Toffler, *Future Shock*, Bodley Head, 1970. Of course, Toffler is right, society is being subjected to violent change but it is not

technological change but social change. Its roots lie in technology only insofar as technology has made possible a massive increase in material well-being and hence personal independence rather than in the direct effects of technological change as such. See J. Roeber, *The Organisation in a Changing Environment*, Addison-Wesley, 1973.

5. Quoted in *The Chemical Economy*, B. G. Reuben and M. L. Burstall, Longman, 1973.

6. *The Juggernauts*, Penguin Books, 1971.

7. Large-scale plants are managerially more convenient (labour troubles apart) than a multiplicity of small ones and also offer more scope for the technical resources of the large organisation. In small organisations large-scale technology is ruled out altogether.

Growth and Pollution: a Programming Approach

*Peter Sadler**

In his paper 'Consumption and Pollution'[2] Dr. Meghnad Desai
of the London School of Economics traces some of the new developments in the Theory of Consumption which lay stress on the
technology of consumption and the way in which the consumer can
achieve levels of satisfaction in various ways by using different
combinations of goods to provide certain groups of characteristics
from which in turn he obtains utility or satisfaction. In this he
follows Lancaster[4] but he develops the Lancaster theme to show
that whereas the earlier orthodox economic approach to the theory
of consumption was atomistic in that total welfare was deemed to be
the sum of individual welfare which in turn was derived from
individual consumption, we ought now to be considering the
external social consequences of individual consumption and including these in the economic calculus which the individualistic approach
does not permit. The conclusion to be drawn from this part of his
argument is that where one can obtain the same level of satisfaction
from different groups of characteristics then that group of characteristics obtained from a combination of goods which provides the
minimum social 'bad' is to be socially desired and society should
so manage its economic activity either by taxation or legislation to
ensure that economic activity of individuals would result in the
desired social combination of outputs.

Desai then goes on in the second half of his paper to develop the
material balance approach[1] and to justify its integration with the
work of Lancaster. This approach, favoured by the ecologist,
stresses the law of the conservation of matter and leads to the conclusion that if economic growth requires the transformation of more

---

* Professor, Director of the Institute for the Study of Sparsely Populated
  Areas, University of Aberdeen. This chapter is an abridged version of the
  original paper.

  E

and more of the world's resources into 'goods' for consumption, the limited ability of the earth to absorb the waste or to transform it must inevitably imply that the utility acquired from these goods produced must eventually be outweighed by the social disutility of the 'bads' derived from the pollution and waste created. By referring to the two approaches, he proceeds to demonstrate that the 'nil growth' approach as at present advocated will in no way guarantee a halt, let alone a reduction in pollution levels, for consumers will inevitably change the combinations of goods that they consume in order to obtain groups of characteristics they require, and this is just as likely to lead to an increase in pollution as would an addition to growth. He argues, therefore, that a nil growth approach is fundamentally ill-founded, and that instead a more correct economic calculus should be sought which will allow a society to take into consideration the effect on the environment, or on what the material balance advocates would term the natural system, of changes in the economic system.

The present paper is a development of the Desai arguments, but relies on arguments derived from welfare theory rather than in his case from the theory of consumption. The paper then develops a method of choice of activities on a macro basis which it is suggested would further the plea that he makes for a pricing system which is more nearly representative of the social valuation of varying types of output than that derived from the present method of atomistic bargaining. It must be stressed, however, that this is not an alternative pricing approach, but is instead a suggestion for a guide for policy to enable policy-makers to intervene in the market and bring individual atomistic prices more in conformity with a structure of prices which would represent social values.

The early welfare economists relied heavily on the approach developed by Pareto, in which an improvement in welfare could only be guaranteed when the gainer could be made better off without making anyone worse off. This approach has been very pervasive in the literature, and has been extremely influential in policy. It is often justified also on the grounds that in any situation where some are made better off and others worse off, judgement of the total effect is impossible because it involves the necessity of inter-personal comparisons. It is an approach that has great appeal in Western society where individual rights are one of the corner-stones of social organisation, and are jealously guarded by the law. Only in circumstances where general benefits can so overwhelmingly be greater than individual costs does our type of society normally interfere with individual liberty, and then compensation is almost always paid. Yet the very concept of society, as a set of interrelationships between its members, implies that it is difficult to envisage many cases in which someone is not made even a little worse off by the betterment of others, especially when it is an imposed change rather than a change which is arrived at by individual bargaining.

Later welfare theorists have adopted some variation of the compensation principle mainly deriving from Kaldor[3]. This approach attempts to avoid the problems of inter-personal comparisons and utilises the view that under circumstances in which some are made worse off while others are made better off, society as a whole is better off if the gainers can compensate the losers for their loss and still have some benefit left over. In many ways modern antagonists to change seem to rely, albeit unconsciously, on a Pareto type of approach, while of course, those who support a given change rely upon the compensation approach. When adjudicating between the two, Government is usually torn between the needs for economic efficiency and the maintenance of individual rights, but in the debate on pollution and growth there is a further application of the Pareto criterion which seems to have passed unnoticed and yet is of crucial importance. For example, it is generally agreed that complete purity of the atmosphere is impossible to obtain, and indeed is unnecessary. But acceptable levels of pollution are usually contained in restrictive legislation. Suppose that an area has already reached the acceptable level of air pollution, and that a company wishes to establish a new factory in the area which, if allowed to operate uncontrolled, would add to the level of pollution. Two alternatives are usually available to the owners of the new factory, either abate the pollution or, occasionally, in some instances, it may be possible to compensate the society in the area in order that they might abate the pollution themselves. (This is often the case in other types of pollution such as aircraft noise where compensation is paid to provide individual sound-proofing.) Given the alternatives, economic efficiency is served by adopting the cheaper, in terms of resource use, of the two alternatives. Yet a third choice is rarely considered, i.e. whether it is feasible to reduce the air pollution created by some other activity in order to make room for the new entrant and still maintain the acceptable level. Thus, under the constraint of a given level of pollution, one in reality needs a choice mechanism which would allow all three alternatives to be taken into account. In fact, what is needed is an approach which will provide an opportunity cost for various types of pollution as soon as a new activity is available. In this way we would be conforming with Desai's plea that the safe-guarding of the natural system should be integrated into the economic approach, and that the correct price weightings should be used to allow proper choice to be made. We need to ascertain the cost of producing each item of current production under both pollution-free and unrestricted conditions, and fit these into a programme model so that the 'shadow price' of each type of pollution would be generated. This type of approach will have the added advantage that society would be able to provide its outputs under the constraints imposed by the requirements of the natural system and given effect in legislation, and at the same time would be achieving this by using the minimum quantities of the earth's resources. Once the 'cheapest' combination of outputs under the restraints have been established, such a method would throw up the shadow prices which, when compared with the market prices would be the limits within which Government could operate its taxation and subsidy system in order to bring prices in the market-place in line with the price structure desired.

An adaptation of the Leontief input-output system will help us to provide both these types of prices as follows.[5]

a_{11}	a_{1m}	$a_{1(m+1)}$	a_{1n}		A_{11}	A_{12}
a_{m1}	a_{mm}	$a_{m(m+1)}$	a_{mn}	OR		
$a_{(m+1)1}$	$a_{(m+1)m}$	$a_{(m+1)(m+1)}$	$a_{(m+1)n}$		A_{21}	A_{22}
a_{n1}	a_{nm}	$an_{(m+1)}$	a_{nn}			
v_1	v_m	v_{m+1}	v_n		$v_1 \ldots v_m$	$v_{m+1} \ldots v_n$

where a_{ij} = input of good i per unit of output of good j
                                    (ij = 1 ... m)

a_{ig} =   „   „   „   „   „   „   „ pollutant of g eliminated by
                                    sector g (g = (m+1) ... n)

a_{gi} = output of pollutant g per unit of output of good i

a_{gk} =   „   „   „   „   „   „   „ pollutant k eliminated
                                    (k = (m+1) ... n)

Thus the a_{ij} matrix (A_{11}) is the usual input-output matrix

the a_{1g} matrix (A_{12}) is the matrix of input requirements for
pollution elimination

the a_{gi} matrix (A_{21}) is the matrix of pollution created per unit
of output

the a_{gk} matrix (A_{22}) is the matrix of pollution created by
pollution elimination

$v_1 \ldots v_m$ is the value added vector for output of goods $1 \ldots m$

$v_{(m+1)} \ldots v_n$ is the value added vector for pollution
elimination actiivity
$(m+1) \ldots n$

Following the usual method, $(1 - A_{11})^{-1}$ will provide the total direct
and indirect requirements on industry i for each unit of final demand
in industry j. But, in production of j, pollution is created, and A_{21}
$(1 - A_{11})^{-1}$ shows the direct and indirect output of each pollutant g
per unit of final demand for the output of the jth industry, $A_{12}A_{21}$
$(1 - A_{11})^{-1}$ will give us the requirement for the elimination of that
pollution. Thus, gross output in a pollution-free situation would be
divided between the indirect requirements (A_{11})., the pollution
elimination requirements $[A_{12}A_{21}(1 - A_{11})^{-1}]$ and final demand.

$$X = A_{11}X + A_{12}A_{21} (1 - A_{11})^{-1} X + Y \quad \ldots\ldots\ldots\ldots\ldots \quad (1)$$
$$X[1 - (A_{11} + A_{-2}A_{21} (1 - A_{11})^{-1})] = Y \quad \ldots\ldots\ldots\ldots\ldots \quad (2)$$
$$X = [1 - (A_{11} + A_{12}A_{21} (1 - A_{11})^{-1})]^{-1} Y \quad \ldots\ldots\ldots\ldots \quad (3)$$

The inverted matrix on the RHS of (3) gives us the direct and
indirect requirements for the production of a unit of each of the jth
outputs in a pollution-free situation. With the unit prices of the
inputs and the value added components known, we would be able
to price the costs of 'pollution free' production of each item in the
final demand vector. If the new technology or product were introduced into the system we would have pollution-free price for that
also. We now have data which allow us to make an extra type of
choice more in keeping with the general equilibrium approach to
economics, and which can be used to find a programming type of
solution.

The problem can be stated as 'minimise the cost of the production of the new output in terms of extra inputs used and outputs
forgone, subject to the constraint that no increase in pollution
levels will take place'.

In this way we would be able to rearrange our production processes to take the maximum advantage from growth, and would be choosing the correct activity from the environmental point of view. Also, if it were decided to reduce an existing level of one form of pollution the same approach can be taken to find the real costs of output foregone (if it means a reduction of output) or extra resources used to produce under conditions of reduced pollution.

Now I am painfully aware that the finding of information for such an approach is, to say the least, a tall order! Yet a disaggregated regional approach could improve, rather than detract from, final solutions. For example, it might prove worthwhile in a national model to install a pollution abatement plant in industry A to permit an increase in output of industry B, but this would be a poor solution if industry A were located exclusively in Scotland and B in Northern Ireland. It would be far better to collect data on a small regional basis and to build up a series of small matrices which could allow independent, regional optimisation to take place, but with a central policy on general pollution levels in order to prevent competitive bidding up of 'prices' of industrial development by competitive lowering of pollution standards.

References

(1) Ayres, R. V. & Kneese, A. V. 'Production, Consumption, and Externalities', *American Economic Review*, June 1969.
(2) Desai, M. Proceedings of seminar on 'The Consumer Society', University of Edinburgh, 30 May–1 June 1973. Tavistock Press (forthcoming).
(3) Kaldor, W. 'Welfare Propositions in Economics and Interpersonal Comparisons of Utility', *Economic Journal*, 1939.
(4) Lancaster, K. 'A New Approach to Consumer Theory', *Journal of Political Economy*, 1966.
(5) Leontief, W. and Ford, D. 'Air Pollution and the Economic Structure' in *Input-Output Techniques*, Brody & Carter (eds.), North Holland Publishing Company, 1972.

Change in Practice

5

The Sociological Analysis of Change

*J. E. T. Eldridge**

1 Introduction

Anyone seriously interested in studying organisations soon discovers
an eclectic mixture of concepts, theories and disciplines, all pur-
porting to offer a contribution to our understanding. The purposes
of the investigators may often be quite different. But however
academic and detached such studies may be, there is no doubt that
directly or indirectly the knowledge attained can have public and
policy relevance when we consider questions which throw light on
organisation processes. This is because the issues of how to understand and control organisations inevitably start to surface. These
issues are inextricably linked with attempts to explain and identify
the problem of organisational change. In this paper I want to cut
a swathe through some of the sociological contributions and per-
spectives. I am conscious of the fact that my audience today is
primarily one of economists and I hope therefore that we will see
some advantages in and connections between our intellectual
division of labour.

For the purposes of exposition, I am going to look first at some
of the attempts made to understand and conceptualise organisations
as entities and secondly, at ways of defining and interpreting
relations between organisations. Empirically, these questions are
linked together. Conceptually, although in somewhat different ways,
they raise for us the problem of pluralist analysis.

2 Organisations as complex entities

I suspect that Roethlisberger and Dickson's *Management and the*

* Professor of Sociology, University of Glasgow. In preparing this paper I
have drawn upon a forthcoming book, *A Sociology of Organisations* by
J. E. T. Eldridge and A. D. Crombie, Allen & Unwin.

Worker is more widely referred to than read these days. Part of its enduring value is, in my opinion, its impressive delineation of the organisation as an entity embodying plural and interacting social systems, which was a definite advance over the earlier Taylorian scientific management analysis. The Hawthorne studies, as the textbooks remind us, contrasted formal organisational demands with informal group behaviour. But they did more than that. Major distinctions are drawn between:

(1) The technical organisation of an enterprise i.e. the organisation of raw materials, tools and machines for accomplishing the productive task.

(2) The human organisation. This is interpreted at the level of the individual members who come to their jobs with varying needs and expectations, which are viewed as a product of personal biography and social conditioning together with social relationships within and outside the plant.

(3) The social organisation. This refers to the occupational and group categories which may be discerned in an enterprise and the patterned relationships emerging from interaction. The relationships, although they may become standardised and even depend on stereotyped conceptions of 'the other', can also be complex and allow of fine gradations. For example the relationship between a foreman and his subordinate may vary depending on whether or not the manager is present. Roethlisberger and Dickson might be ethnomethodologists before the term was coined when they write:

> These subtle nuances of relationships are so much a part of everyday life that they are commonplace. They are taken for granted. The vast amount of social conditioning that has taken place by means of which a person manoeuvres himself gracefully through the intricacies of these finely shaded social distinctions is seldom explicitly realised. Attention is paid only when a new social situation arises where the past social training of the person prevents him from making the necessary delicate interpretations of a given social signal and hence brings forth the 'socially wrong' response.[1]

(4) The formal organisation. This is a prescriptive set of rules, policies and procedures which purport to lay down what the goals of the enterprise are and how the members are to relate to one another in order to realise the defined objectives. These rules will be of a prescriptive nature and will seek to provide the grounds for a control system to secure the co-operation of the organisation's members.

(5) The informal organisation. Behaviour in organisations cannot be captured in formal statements about the ways in which fuctional groups are supposed to relate for technical and production purposes. There are other bases upon which individuals and groups are differentiated and evaluated. The various work groups studies at Hawthorne unearthed important examples of just such informal organisations and provided the impetus to many other such studies subsequently.

(6) The ideological organisation. The concern here is with the system of beliefs and values which may be located in an organisation. These may be general throughout an organisation, or they may be conected with particular segments of the organisation, formal or informal. Examples of the kinds of value systems Roethlisberger and Dickson have in mind are: the logic of cost—the set of ideas concerning the evaluation of the economic purposes of the organisation; the logic of efficiency—ideas as to how to maximise the collaborative efforts of organisations' members to achieve efficiency; and the logic of sentiments—the values placed on human relationships within and between particular groups. What is interesting here is the sense of a plurality of belief systems co-existing within the organisation, different in range, intensity and content and certainly not always complementary. One tries to discuss what their beliefs are, how and why they are appropriated and what connection they have with reality (this last on the assumption that the investigator can check out on what constitutes reality).

> Some of these ideas and beliefs represent more closely the actual situation than others. In all cases, however, they are abstractions from the concrete situation. In this respect they are to the concrete situation as maps are to the territories they represent, and like maps these abstractions may be either misleading or useful. They may be misleading because sometimes the person using them fails to realise they are representing only one part of the total organisation. Sometimes in the minds of certain individuals these abstractions tend to become divorced from the social reality and in effect, lead an independent existence.[2]

What is of interest about the kind of differentiation of organisational elements noted above is, first, the strong sense of the need to appreciate the interconnectedness of the parts of the organisation. Although the matter need not detain us in this context, we may briefly observe that the starting points for charting changes in relationships between the parts are two-fold. Outside the organisation is the economic problem—how does it adjust to meet changing market situations? Inside the organisation is the matter of changes in the technical system. The investigators note, for example, the possibility of disparities in the rates of change in technical systems and social organisations. Since the ideological organisation of the plant is interlaced with the technical, human and social organisations, the ramifications in terms of conflict and co-operation in the enterprise are extensive and complex.

The second point of interest is that the implications of this kind of analysis were spelled out with reference to managerial control. If management wished to control the direction of organisational activity then, the argument ran, it must first understand the pluralistic nature of the enterprise. Roethlisberger and Dickson essentially posed the question, how can organisational effectiveness be achieved? This question is directed at management and an answer along the following lines is suggested:

(1) Do not have an over-simple view of how to control an organisation. 'Scientific controls have been introduced to further the economic purpose of the concern and of the individuals within it. Much of this advance has gone on in the name of efficiency or rationalisation. Nothing comparable to this advance has gone on in the development of skills and techniques for securing co-operation, that is for getting individuals and groups of individuals working together effectively and with satisfaction to themselves.'[3]

(2) Do not have an unrealistic or faulty ideology, Recognise, for example, the reality of informal organisation both at worker and management level. Do not condemn this as 'bad' or attempt to eradicate such organisation since this is impossible; rather consider how it may facilitate purposive co-operation and communication. Sectional interests can be transcended in this way: 'What the Relay Assembly Test Room experiment showed was that when innovations are introduced carefully and with regard to the natural sentiments of the workers, the workers are likely to develop a spontaneous type of informal organisation which will not only express more adequately their own values and significance but is also more likely to be in harmony with the aims of management.'[4]

Consequently the pluralist analysis of the enterprise moves to a prescriptive statement about how the organisation as a whole might more effectively be controlled by management through the operation of a human relations ideology. This is done on the grounds of realism. The authenticity of management is thus legitimated on the grounds that, through collaboration with all groups, management is acting in the interests of all organisation members. The true interests of management, based on a realistic appraisal of the pluralistic character of the enterprise are identical with the true interests of the constituent groups. This seems a good example therefore of how social analysis can come in practice to be a form of managerial sociology in the way in which it is interpreted and utilised, although logically the analysis can be separated from the interpretation.

This emphasis on the need for managerial ideologies to be realistic has also more recently been explicitly articulated by Fox.[5] In his discussion of industrial organisation he poses this question:

> What is the closest analogy to the enterprise—is it, or ought it to be, analogous to a team, unified by a common purpose, or is it more plausibly viewed as a coalition of interests, a miniature democratic State composed of sectional groups with divergent interests over which the Government tries to maintain some kind of dynamic equilibrium?[6]

He suggests that the way we answer the question affects the way we expect people to behave or ought to behave, how we respond to their actual behaviour in the organisation. Further it will also affect our prescriptions as to how to change behaviour we regard as inappropriate. It is perhaps as well to note that 'we' in the above sentence, primarily refers to managers, as does the term Government in the quotation.

Fox then contrasts the unitary and pluralist conceptions of the industrial enterprise and suggests that many managers hold a unitary view which is, he argues, demonstrably at variance with the facts. In pursuing his analysis Fox is concerned to demonstrate the reality of conflicts of interests in the enterprise and the existence of competing sources of authority for employees' allegiances both within and without the enterprise. Against this he sets unitary managerial ideologies which interpret conflict in terms of personalities, or failure in communication, or agitators who are 'rocking the boat' and which treat co-operation in the enterprise as axiomatic and consequently do not examine the assumption it contains.

Yet the analysis of pluralism is addressed to managers who through understanding the pluralist nature of the enterprise may be able more effectively to control and change it:

> A management which fully accepts the reality of work-group interests which conflict quite legitimately with their own will seek honestly and patiently to understand the causes of particular

group practices and policies, in the full awareness that
imaginative understanding is a precondition of success in
modifying behaviour.[7]

And again in commenting on restrictive practices and workers'
resistance to change he says:

> Only a pluralistic view can see them for what they are: rational
> responses by sectional interests to protect employment, stabilise
> earnings, maintain job status, defend group bargaining power or
> preserve craft boundaries. The unitary view can condemn them
> as morally indefensible: the pluralistic view can understand them,
> and by understanding is in a position to change them.[8]

The discussion then centres around the idea of transcending conflicts of interest by moving to a higher level of mutual advantage.
Yet such advantages, while mutual, need not be evenly distributed
nor for that matter need they be total. What is under discussion is
how the Government (established management) can continue to
govern, given competing sources of authority. And the pluralistic
analysis is put forward as a more realistic way of proceeding. Within
that context 'the managerial method in future must increasingly be
that of winning consent of work-groups through the medium of
ordered relationships with those groups; relationships which recognise their independence and their right to express it through their
own leaders'.[9] It is important to add that Fox's general analysis of
pluralism has significantly shifted since that paper was written.[10]
    I should like now to take two further examples, both of which I
think are analytically more sophisticated than those so far mentioned. First, there is Gouldner's treatment of functional autonomy
within organisations. By way of critique he attacks 'rational'
models of organisation because of what one might now term a unitary perspective. This views the organisation as a structure of
manipulable parts which may be modified to achieve organisational
efficiency by careful planning and decision-making. In essence it
assumes a view as to what constitutes efficiency and desirable
long-term objectives and conviction that the parts of the organisation can be brought into conformity with the plan. Such a model, we
may note, may be constructed by social scientists and may obviously
provide hope to those in organisations who are in positions of
authority and are looking for a theoretical base for their prescriptive activities. Gouldner is, however, also dissatisfied with what he
terms the natural system model of organisations. This is a model
based on the assumption of the organisation striving to survive

and maintain its equilibrium. This focus on the organisation as the unit of analysis can, in Gouldner's view, emphasise homeostatic mechanisms and the emergent normative structures with an accompanying view of shared organisational values. Independent action and the possibility of a plurality of values within the organisation is consequently minimised.

Part of Gouldner's argument is that both of these models are inadequate as total approaches to organisational analysis and that more conceptual subtlety is called for. The notion of functional autonomy for example 'directs attention to the fact that *some* parts may survive separation from others, that parts vary in their dependence upon one another, and that their interdependence is not necessarily symmerical'.[11] This is a modifying statement about natural systems which does not take for granted the mutual interdependence of the parts of an organisation. Asymmetry as well as symmetry may be detected. Thus one may examine what parts of an organisation may survive in times of crises and what parts may be pared down or disappear. In a business organisation, in times of cut-back, research and development or welfare functions may prove to be more vulnerable than production functions. But conceptually the unitary/pluralism polarity becomes a matter of centripetal versus centrifugal forces:

> Assuming that the organisation's parts, no less than the organisation as a whole, operate to maintain their boundaries and to remain in equilibrium, then the parts should be expected to defend their functional autonomy, or at least some measure of it from encroachment. This suggests that a basic source of organisational tension may derive, on the one hand, from the tendency of the parts to resist encroachment on their functional autonomy and, on the other, from contrary tendencies of the organisation's controlling centre to limit or reduce the functional autonomy of the parts. The widely noted tensions between field officers and main officers, as well as the common organisational oscillation between centralisation and decentralisation seem to support this assumption, as do the frequently observed rejection of 'close supervision' and the pressure which almost all role players exert to maintain some social distance from and freedom from control by those most crucially concerned with their work.[12]

The importance of this kind of presentation is that conflict is built into the analysis, based upon competition between the parts and between the whole and the parts, and upon the postulate of asymmetrical relationships within the system. Hence assumptions

about agreed organisational goals, or about strains towards organisational equilibrium cannot remain unexamined. The empirical question becomes how much functional autonomy may be observed in
particular organisations and how is this to be explained. Thus high
functional autonomy suggests a form of pluralist organisation and
low functional autonomy a more unitary one. Another important
example at this level of our exposition is Burns's significantly titled
paper 'On the Plurality of Social Systems'.[13] Burns shares with
Gouldner doubts about the adequacy of rationality models of the
organisation. Yet a resurgent interest in formal organisations has,
in his opinion, tended to bring back into focus classical management theory conceptions of unitary structures and his critical
comments are on similar lines to those of Gouldner. However, his
analytical response is not in terms of functional autonomy of sub-
systems in relation to the overall organisational system: rather he
postulates the existence of distinct social systems which are inter-
related in an organisational milieu. In a business enterprise, for
example, he differentiates three such systems: the working orgnisa-
tion, the career system and the political system. Each of these
supposes individuals and groups in competition with each other, in
an arena where ground rules exist but are themselves challenged
from time to time. A plurality of means-ends systems for achieving
certain posts may co-exist for the individual. This will be reflected
and represented in the social relationships and conduct of the
individual organisation members. Over and against the unitary view,
which would treat the working organisation as central and other
relationships as deviant, Burns argues for the necessary pluralism of
the organisation and consequently contends that the political system
and career structure necessarily influence the character of the
working organisation. This is so whether or not the ideology of
the organisation is based upon unitary or pluralist premises. The
methodological question becomes, in Burns's analysis, to discern
the patterns of individual commitments in order to account for the
particular mixture of co-operation and conflict in the organisation.
The general point about the relationship between the individual and
the organisation in this pluralist conceptual analysis is well brought
out in the following comment:

> The interaction of all these systems rests on the fact that an
> individual may invoke any of them as the dominant reference
> system for this or that action, decision or plan, even though
> an outside observer, or the individual himself, for that matter,
> may see other manifest relevance of what he is doing to all or any
> of the other systems. What I have called systems exist for the

individual as social *Gestalten*, without which acts cannot be seen as items in means-end or cause-effect change, and decisions cannot be given any preference ordering.[14]

3 Relationships between organisations: pluralism, participation and change

In labelling relationships between organisations as pluralistic one encounters the fact that this sometimes has reference to particular kinds or organisations, say religious, and sometimes to a whole complex of organisations in society, say religious, political, military, economic and legal. There is one general point which may be made at the outset. It is that there is an implied contrast between a monopolistic organisation and organisations that are in competition with each other. The nature and degree of that competition invites much more specific examination. The extreme contrast, drawing upon economic terminology, is between a total monopoly on the one hand and an organisation operating in conditions of perfect competition in a designated market situation.

It may be recalled that when Joseph Schumpeter wrote *Capitalism, Socialism and Democracy*, he constructed a theory of political competition which was derived from the economic concept of competition. He did not, however, imagine that a situation of perfect competition could be realised, but he does make the following comment: 'Between this ideal case which does not exist and the cases in which all competition with the established leader is prevented by force, there is a continuous range of variations within which the democratic method of government shades off into the autocratic one by imperceptible steps.'[15] In the political sphere, therefore, the contrast is drawn between autocracy and democracy and the possibility of imperfections and inequalities in the competitive struggle as between groups is built in. This is an important qualification, for without it the pluralist conception of political activity is liable to be presented as an equilibrating process in which organisations of roughly equal strength achieve parity in the distribution and exercise of power. Such an assumption, if permitted, tends to justify whatever outcomes occur in the competitive struggle as democratic. But this assumes what has to be proved and, as Miliband has suggested:

> What is wrong with pluralist-democratic theory is not its insistence on the factor of competition but its claim (very often its implicit assumption) that, the major organised 'interests' in these societies, and notably capital and labour, compete on

F

more or less equal terms, and that none of them is therefore
able to achieve a decisive and permanent advantage in the process
of competition. This is where ideology enters and turns
observation into myth.[16]

The above quotation touches also on the question of the relationship between the strictly political sphere and other spheres of social
life. For the moment, however, one proceeds to reflect on the fact
that the pattern of competition between organisations is one thing
and the pattern of competition of individuals and groups within
organisations another. This is implied in Figure 1.

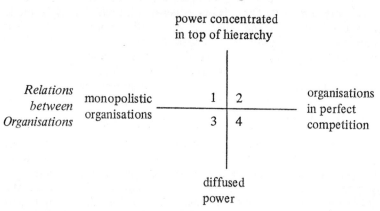

As soon as one cross-cuts the power dimension in organisations
with the market situation of organisations the distinction between
elitist and participatory forms is suggested. Accordingly, organisational arrangements falling in sections 2 and 4 express pluralistic
relationships: the former however are elitist and the latter participatory. Because of his view of the nature of political parties in
large-scale societies, Schumpeter's own emphasis was on elitist
pluralism as the only effective and realistic way to approximate
democracy. By a simple semantic manoeuvre one is able to equate
democracy with elitist pluralism. If, however, one applied the
scheme to political parties (and allowing that in reality we are
dealing with continuous variables) one might label the four sections
as follows: (1) one-party dictatorship; (2) multi-party bureaucracies;
(3) one-party democracy; (4) multi-party democracy. An underlying
theme of this kind of arrangement relates to the question of
accountability. This suggests that accountability is maximised where
party diversity in a competitive situation is fused with involvement
of the party members and adherents in the activities of the party.

We can see then that when a set of relationships is labelled as pluralistic the question 'what kind of pluralism?' needs to be asked. Take, for example, organised religion. There the questions of pluralism has been fruitfully pursued by Peter Berger.[17] He points to the monopolistic position which religious establishments have typically enjoyed in society throughout most of human history, in and through which the legitimation of individual and collective life has been obtained. Religious organisations thus constituted regulatory agencies governing thought and action. This treatment of religious monopoly serves as an important contrast with religous pluralism, which Berger defines as follows:

> The key characteristic of all pluralistic situations ... is that religious ex-monopolies can no longer take for granted the allegiance of their client populations. Allegiance is voluntary and thus, by definition, less than certain. As a result, the religious tradition which previously could be authoritatively imposed, now has to be *marketed*. It must be 'sold' to a clientele that is no longer constrained to 'buy'. The pluralistic situation is, above all, a *market situation*. In it, the religious institutions become agencies and the religious traditions become consumer commodities. And at any rate a good deal of religious activity in this situation comes to be dominated by the logic of market economics.[18]

Berger's own main field of illustration here is the USA. There one has a constitutional separation of Church and State (and in that sense a secular society) but a condition of religious toleration permitted by the State. A diversity of religious world views (until the rise of the Black Muslim movement subsumed under Catholic, Protestant and Jew) could be located and were in a competitive relationship with one another. The main emphasis in Berger's analysis is not the experiences of religious differences expressed in the early settlement and frontier situations, rather it is the significance of the growth of denomonationalism. Its significance lies partly in the accompanying growth of bureaucracy. This can lead to certain organisational similarities notwithstanding the theological differences. Even a denomination which, as a matter of doctrine, lays emphasis on local church autonomy may tend to centralise decision-making and co-ordinate its activities through a centralised administration.[19] Now although these denominations may in some sense be in competition with one another for the religious adherence of potential members, and although historically they may earlier have had a sect character and been sharply antagonistic with one another, the bureaucratic pluralism which they now represent has an element of collution about it. The denominational bureaucrats face common problems of membership recruitment, ministerial selection and training, handling problems of finance, investment and the utilisation of resources, and maintaining satisfactory relationships with a range of agencies in government, industry and the social services. In discussion with other denominations the bureaucrats may work out territorial agreements both at home and in missionary situations. The common concern of the bureaucrats for results and a common administrative mentality does supply an important clue to the ecumenical movement. This, as Berger rightly points out, has much of the character of cartelisation about it. There is a process of guided mergers and an attempt to organise the market by agreement:

> Both within and beyond Protestantism there has been increasing consultation and collaboration between the large bodies 'surviving' the merger process. It is important to see that this process of cartelisation does *not* tend towards the re-establishment of a monopoly situation—in other words, the notion of an eventual 'world church' is unlikely to be realised empirically. Rather, the tendency is oligopolistic with mergers in prospect only to the extent that these are functional in terms of rationalising competition. To go beyond this extent, quite apart from the strain this would put on the theological legitimation, would actually be irrational in terms of the institutional interests of the several religious bureaucracies.[20]

The bureaucratic pluralism noted here is, then, oligopolistic. It should be added that sectarian groupings can and do exist alongside the denominations. Such groupings may have something of a breakaway character emphasising, say, a doctrinal issue or question of ecclesiastical polity. But numerical success tends to set in motion a bureaucratising process, as the Salvation Army in the nineteenth century and the Pentecostal Movement in the twentieth century illustrate. Even groupings which are able to maintain a hostile attitude towards 'the world' and in that respect remain sectarian, such as the Jehovah's Witnesses, are in organisational terms highly bureaucratised administrations.

There is a tendency for bureaucratic organisations by virtue of their hierarchical arrangements to be elitist. Continual comment in the need to liberalise the structures of the Church of Rome or to democratise the organisation of the Church of England is in itself a response to the perceived reality. It is not intended to imply by contrast that sect-type organisations are necessarily democratic; they may be but they may also be highly authoritarian organisations. The discussion of bureaucratic pluralism in the religious sphere prompts one to note that the elitist organisational form and oligopolistic market situation find their parallels in business and trade union organisations and, of course, in the organisation of political parties in modern industrial societies. There is, however, by no means agreement among commentators as to the general significance of this state of affairs. The precise shape of these organisations and the contours of their market situation will be matters of continuing debate and inquiry. But in conceptualising the issue of organisational change at the macro-level in the way that I have, I intended to suggest that creative conversations could be developed between political economists and sociologists. What better tribute could we pay, at a Scottish meeting of the British Association to Adam Smith and Adam Ferguson?

Notes

1. F. T. Roethlisberger and W. T. Dickson, *Management and the Worker*, Wiley, 1964.
2. Ibid., pp. 562–3.
3. Ibid., pp. 552–3.
4. Ibid., pp. 561–2.
5. Alan Fox, *Industrial Sociology and Industrial Relations*, HMSO, 1966.
6. Ibid., p. 2.
7. Ibid., p. 10.
8. Ibid., p. 12.
9. Ibid., p. 14.
10. A. Fox, 'Industrial Relations: A Social Critique of Pluralist Ideology' in John Child (ed.), *Man and Organisation*, Allen and Unwin, 1973, pp. 185–233.
11. A. Gouldner, 'Organisational Analysis' in R. K. Merton *et al.* (eds.) *Sociology Today*, Harper Torchbooks, 1965, p. 419.
12. Ibid., pp. 420–1.
13. T. Burns, 'On the Plurality of Social Systems' in M. Gilbert (ed.), *The Modern Business Enterprise*, Penguin, 1972, pp. 105–21.
14. Ibid., pp. 119–20.
15. J. Schumpeter, *Capitalism, Socialism and Democracy*, Allen and Unwin, 1943, p. 271.
16. R. Miliband, *The State in Capitalist Society*, Weidenfeld and Nicolson, 1969, p. 146.
17. Peter L. Berger, *The Social Reality of Religion*, Faber, 1969.
18. Ibid., p. 137.
19. See for example, Paul Harrison, *Authority and Power in the Free Church Tradition*, Princeton University Press, 1959.
20. Berger, op. cit., p. 143.

6

Arbitrating Industrial Change

*T. L. Johnston**

Industrial relations arbitration in Britain has suffered from a split personality in recent years. On the one hand, there persists the mystique—the Solomon syndrome—which see arbitration, and arbitrators, as the repository of Truth and Wisdom. On the other hand, the arbitration process has of late fallen into some disrepute as a result of succesive governments allegedly using it as a tool in their incomes policy stratagems.

Even before arbitration came to be associated with regulatory machinery of incomes policy, however, the discussion of industrial arbitration in Britain tended to concentrate on its role in the resolution of wage disputes. The literature is admittedly sparse, but much of the discussion, for example that in the 1920s in which Lord Amulree and Dr. Mary Rankin were leading participants, took wages as the main substance of arbitration.[1] Lord Amulree saw the case law of the original Industrial Court as building blocks which would distil principles on wage determination.[2]

This preoccupation, past and present, with arbitration as though it were exclusively, or even primarily, a wage dispute settlement mechanism, has been unfortunate. It has tended to obscure and restrict the scope of thinking about the role that arbitration can and might play in industrial relations. The purpose of this paper is accordingly to widen the perspective on arbitration in Britain. Arbitration is viewed here in a wide context of collective bargaining, and as a device which can be extended beyond wage settlement and a simple fire-fighting role. It will be argued that arbitration can, and indeed ought to have a larger part to play in collective bargaining viewed as a changing and developing phenomenon. Our theme is industrial change and the relevance of arbitration as a device which can promote such change in a useful way.

* Professor of Economics, Heriot-Watt University.

In many countries the analysis of industrial arbitration can proceed on the basis of a clear distinction between 'rights', or interpretation, and 'interest' (new contract) disputes. There is no such
terminological or conceptual framework or shortcut in Britain. In
many countries interest disputes have not generally been regarded
as legitimate game for the arbitrator; by contrast, interpretation
disputes may have to be settled peaceably, and ultimately by arbitrators or by a Labour Court if the parties to collective agreements
cannot resolve their differences on their own or with the aid of
conciliation or mediation. All industrial disputes in Britain can
appear as differences of interest, and perhaps be resolved only by
the ultimate sanction of coercive action, in the context of what
Kahn-Freund has called the 'institutional or dynamic' type of bargaining procedure which he sees the open-ended British scheme of
things as epitomising.[3]
  This distinction between rights and interests may not always be a
clear-cut or useful one. Wedderburn has argued, powerfully and
persuasively, that there is a spectrum of delicate colour from
interests to rights.[4] Not everyone would agree that the colours are
delicate. Yet, to put his point another way, a good many rights
disputes may obviously raise matters of interest. A more subtle
point, to be developed later, is that rights disputes are not always
'one-off' situations or resoluble within the framework of a static
view of the relations between the parties to a collective agreement
that is running its course. Industrial relations do not stand still while
an agreement is in force. Once this point has been accepted, arbitration may have a useful part to play in facilitating change within
the broad context of an agreement. As to interest disputes, it is
important not to equate these solely with wage disputes. Many
other matters besides wages can be comprehended by 'new contract'
negotiations, and on these too arbitration may have something
useful to contribute. So at any rate we shall argue.
  A definition of industrial arbitration is in order before we proceed
further. It may be defined as the resolution of industrial disputes
by the adjudication of a third party, based on the consensual
surrender of economic power by the parties. Its distinguishing
characteristic is that it comes into play *after* negotiations between
the parties, including conciliation/mediation, have been deployed
without success in settling the problem or problems at issue between
the parties. A good deal of debate has taken place as to whether
arbitration is part of the voluntary system of industrial relations,
or a negation of it. The debate is an arid one. The fundamental
point is that arbitration comes 'at the end of the line'. Of course
it is not easy to regard compulsory arbitration as part of the

'voluntary system'. In any case such compulsory experience is
exceptional in Britain, and it will not be considered here. The
position taken here is that voluntary arbitration is part of, and the
last stage in, voluntary collective bargaining machinery.

This position is consistent with the public policy that developed
in Britain under the Conciliation Act of 1896 and the Industrial
Courts Act of 1919, namely that the State provides facilities for
conciliation and arbitration. The latter may be deployed under
official machinery only after the due process of negotiation and
conciliation has been tried and has failed. The new independent
Conciliation and Arbitration Service seems likely to continue this
voluntary framework.

This leads to a consideration of the scale and characteristics of
industrial arbitration in Britain. Arbitration in Britain under the
official machinery has recently been rather sparse, in part because
of the odium which the alleged nobbling of arbitrators for incomes
policy reasons, referred to at the outset, has aroused. In 1973, for
instance, some fifty 'single arbitrations' were carried out by individual arbitrators under the official machinery referred to above
which operated through the Department of Employment. The figure
had been steady for about four years, at about fifty per annum. (In
the course of 1974 business promised (or threatened) to become
brisker, no doubt in part because of the new device of the independent Conciliation and Arbitration Service.) Few (tripartite) Boards
of Arbitration were convened, while the hearings before the original
Industrial Court (now the Industrial Arbitration Board) had been on
the decline for several years. All this is hardly big business on a
large scale. Indeed, most single arbitrations tend to deal with 'little
local difficulties'. The modest use of arbitration has been seen by
some as a tribute to the effectiveness of British collective bargaining.[5]

What is not clear from this picture is the extent of privately
arranged arbitration. Arbitration arranged through the official
channels may be the tip of the iceberg. Certainly, there is plenty
of machinery which lies outside the official networks, though a good
deal of that also uses the good offices of the Department of Employment in enlisting the services of privately appointed arbitrators. But
we do not know the total score for all the industrial arbitrations
conducted in Britain in any year.

As to the characteristics of arbitration in Britain, this can perhaps
best be revealed, or unveiled, by saying something about one's own
experiences as an arbitrator. To bare one's soul in this way is no
doubt to run the risk of becoming an ex-arbitrator; but an arbitrator
is only as good as his last award in any case. Yet it is the writer's

conviction that arbitration in Britain has been ill-served by the cloak of coyness and anonymity that has surrounded it, and this paper is to be viewed in part as an attempt to promote, or provoke, more systematic discussion of the subject in Britain. We are short of information about practicalities, about what actually happens 'at the coal face'. Some (justified) confessions of an arbitrator now follow.

First, it is important to notice that it is the parties to an arbitration application who set the framework for the arbitrator by the terms of reference that they agree. This framework may stem from an agreement, from custom and practice and so forth, and the parties set the scene for the arbitrator within a broad area of their joint intent. It does not follow from this, secondly, that the issue or issues that the arbitrator has to resolve have been identified, narrowed and distilled with great care in the preceding stages of negotiation and conciliation. By accident or design, the terms of reference may conceal as much as they reveal. The obvious point here is that the reported difference may simply constitute the top layer of something deeper.

Thirdly, the evidence or arguments led by the parties, both in the form of written submissions in advance of the hearing and in the verbal, and usually very informal, testimony at the arbitration hearing itself, constitute the substance that puts flesh on the terms of reference. This dialogue, or Inquisition, refines and clarifies the problems for the arbitrator. It is a process which may provide the rationale for the arbitrator doing what critics of arbitration frequently regard as something reprehensible, namely 'splitting the difference'. Dr. Rankin suggested that splitting the difference was to be seen as part of the process of accommodation.

> More generally he will follow the principle of safety and steer a middle course between the rival claims, arriving at what is in reality a conciliatory decision, i.e. he will give no definite interpretation to the principle (of what the industry can bear), but will be guided in each case by the facts placed before him and the views of the parties concerned; he will arrive at a decision not essentially different to that which the parties themselves with their own knowledge of demand and supply could, given greater confidence or reasonableness, have arrived at by agreement. This procedure is frequently somewhat contemptuously referred to as 'splitting the difference', but in splitting the difference under such circumstances the Arbitrator is in reality applying a principle voluntarily agreed upon by the parties before him though the agreement be by implication only.[6]

This comment on 'splitting the difference' perhaps implies that the difference is a wage one, and that only one difference exists. To stop at that conclusion would be to defeat the point of this paper. There may be more than one issue to resolve in fact, if not in the explicit terms of reference. The question of 'tradeoffs' between the positions of the parties then arises, and at arbitration has to be resolved.

It is important to notice, next, that an arbitration hearing is not a divorce proceeding. Rather it is the opposite, in the sense that the parties have to live together after the award has been made. In this respect the arbitration process can frequently serve a therapeutic or cleansing purpose. Put another way, arbitrators delude themselves if they imagine that disputes are passed to them because the parties lack skill to resolve their problems on their own. The arbitrator is not infrequently a whipping boy, and at the end of many an arbitration hearing it is the arbitrator who retires with the weight of the glum world on his shoulders, and with a decision to be made, while the parties, having passed the buck, may depart together 'With peace and consolation. . . . And calm of mind, all passion spent.'

The fundamental practical proposition to be argued here, however, is that *continuity* of the industrial relationships is germane to arbitration hearings and decisions. However narrow the issue to be determined, it may by implication contain the seeds of change, both in the argument of the parties and in the award itself. The solution that the arbitrator finds to the problem of Today may carry forward into the future, and not least if the parties dislike the award and seek at some appropriate future moment to be rid of it. Explicitly, too, the parties at arbitration may seek guidance from the arbitrator, or they may indicate how they wish or propose to conduct their relationships on the disputed subject in the future. In one way or another, therefore, the arbitrator may comment on problems and make suggestions, instead of confining himself to the narrow interpretation of his terms of reference.

Critics may see such deviations from the Path of Righteousness as an unwarranted departure from the judicial function of the arbitration process. Yet, as Sir Roy Wilson, doyen of arbitrators, has pointed out, the analogy between a judge in a court of law and an arbitrator is not a complete one, in that industrial arbitrators 'are intended to have, and to bring to the performance of their task, an experience of the facts of industrial life extending far beyond the facts of any particular case'.[7] What can this mean, if not that the arbitrator takes a wide view of the situation into which parties have introduced him, and that in being equitable he need not be legal?

Agreements arrived at through the process of collective bargaining are some kind of whole. Without stretching too far the use of that much abused but suggestive word 'organic', it has to be recognised that each part of the industrial relations nexus affects other parts, and a decision taken as to one part of the relationship may require consequential adjustments of others.

This theme of *continuity* can be discerned very clearly in the subjects of single arbitration awards in a typical recent year. There were disputes about shiftwork, bonus payments, salary increases, the method of calculation of overtime pay, none of which could be regarded as culminating in a simple 'one-off' solution that was devoid of implications for the future. The same can be said of other differences, on such matters as whether the national agreement applied, whether there had been adequate consultation, the inclusion of merit payments in minimum earnings levels, and the interpretation of a manpower productivity agreement.

The arbitrator may thus find himself, consciously or unwittingly, solving a present problem which carries into the future. Even if he is endeavouring to confine his award, the continuity of the industrial relationship may not permit this. Of course this is not to argue that arbitrators should seek to stray from their terms of reference by taking the whole scheme of relations between the parties to be their province. That would be absurd. What is being pleaded for here is the recognition that arbitration takes place in a context and a continuing one at that.

Our theme of a more open stance towards arbitration leads naturally to the question whether arbitrators should give reasons for their awards. Lord Amulree did seek to make reasoned awards the cornerstone of his endeavour to build up a body of industrial relations jurisprudence (mainly on wage principles) from the cases which the original Industrial Court determined. More recently, the subject was aired when Sir Roy Wilson gave evidence before the Donovan Commission. It was interested in reasoned awards primarily in the context of incomes policy, and was haunted by the thought that one would never be able to tell whether arbitrators were playing to the rules of an incomes policy game if they did not give reasons. Hence the Commission's recommendation that arbitrators should be encouraged to make reasoned awards.[8]

The objection raised against this was that the independence and integrity of an arbitrator might be prejudiced if he had to look over his shoulder at some incomes policy instruction. Much more disappointing in the dialogue between Donovan and Wilson, however, was that no one probed in any depth the possible role of arbitration in disputes that did not directly concern wage policy issues, and even on the subject of reasoned wage awards the emphasis was entirely cautious and negative.

Sir Roy Wilson suggested that the Industrial Court 'not infrequently' did give reasons, where it felt that 'this would help to make clear the real meaning and intention of the award or to prevent misunderstanding or any unintended chain reaction . . .' But in the great majority of awards by arbitrators 'the decision is set out without any reasons or discussion of the merits of the rival submissions put forward by the parties'. The case against reasoned awards fell under two main heads. First, the arbitration was meant to terminate a controversial episode and to give reasons could prolong or even exacerbate the differences between the parties. Second, the giving of reasons would to some extent result in the building up of a body of case law, and this could create excessive rigidity.[9]

These fears appear somewhat exaggerated. On the first, everyone would accept that on occasion it is wise to Let Sleeping Dogs Lie, and not wash dirty linen in public. These are matters in which judgement is certainly needed. Yet the emphasis was negative and retrospective, instead of positive and constructive. Nor need the second fear, that of precedents, be given such prominence. The US system of industrial arbitration succeeds in grounding arbitration awards on the foundation that each is resolving a particular dispute in its own context. Whether parties to a dispute or other people seek to use precedents or generalise from an award is an entirely separate question.

The US system makes much use of case reporting, and arbitrators carry on a running dialogue about their work. There seems more to be gained from this open stance than from a clandestine attitude which is reluctant to put reasoned awards in the shop window. Paradoxically too, the very predominance of *ad hoc* single arbitrations in Britain makes it easier to avoid the fears that arbitrators may be tempted to make 'case law' if they reveal their reasons for awards.

The references to industrial arbitration in the USA encourage us to look more closely at some of its main features.[10] There the arbitration of interpretation or rights disputes has developed as a major service to industry. Private voluntary arbitration developed substantially in the course of the Second World War and expanded afterwards on the initiative of the collective bargaining parties. Although the Labor Management Relations Act (Taft-Hartley Act) of 1947 made collective agreements legally enforceable in the Courts it also declared (Sec. 203 (d)) that

Final adjustment by a method agreed upon by the parties is hereby declared to be the desirable method for settlement of grievance disputes arising over the application or interpretation of an existing collective-bargaining agreement.

The declaration confirmed rapidly developing practice, and arbitration has come to feature in well over 90 per cent of collective agreements as the final step in grievance procedures.

The operation of this system, with its mixture of legally enforceable agreements and private arbitration, provides a most useful corrective to those who seek to equate labour law with the intervention of the Courts, and the interpretation of legal documents with legalism. In the famous Steel Trilogy cases of 1960 the US Supreme Court encouraged the use of private grievance arbitration and sought to avoid the Courts developing into appellate bodies on arbitrators' awards. Broadly, it supported the use of arbitration as a creative remedy in interpretation disputes, while at the same time making it clear that an arbitration award has to draw its essence from the collective bargaining agreement. The agreement sets the context, and an arbitrator does not sit to dispense his own brand of industrial justice.

The National Labor Relations Board, one of the custodians of national labour policy in the USA, has also developed a reasonable *modus vivendi* with arbitration. On the question whether it would look favourably on interfering with arbitrators' awards if these were alleged to have violated the Labor Management Relations Act, the NLRB has evolved a policy of self-restraint. In 1955 it enunciated the Spielberg doctrine, indicating that it would not independently decide any case that had been determined by an arbitrator as long as three conditions were satisfied: the arbitration proceedings appeared to have been fair and regular; the parties agreed to accept the award as final and binding; and the arbitrator's decision was not clearly repugnant to the purposes and policies of the Board. A fourth principle was later advanced (in the Raytheon case) which requires arbitrators to show that they have considered any statutory rights which a party may have claimed.

The US experience has also focused a number of issues. First, what is arbitrable? The basic proposition is that a grievance is not arbitrable only if the parties have specifically excluded it. This practice has led to the question of exclusions becoming an issue in new contract negotiations. A related matter is the occurrence of strikes in the course of a contract. Most agreements contain no-strike clauses, but many of them do permit strikes in certain limited circumstances over specified matters. About one-third of strikes in the USA are estimated to occur during the term of agreements, though it appears that they cover only about 10 per cent of the man days lost.

Other features of US industrial arbitration are that it relies heavily on single arbitrators, and often on a hard core of experienced or known arbitrators. Typically they give reasons for their awards and a considerable information system has developed, through the publication of awards and via public discussion of arbitration. Of late the private arbitration industry has been criticised on the ground of delay and high cost. There is much mythology, and some factual information, about the fees and expenses of arbitrators and of the parties themselves. One recent critic has deplored what he calls the legalism of the 'transcript trauma'.[11]

Overall, however, the US experience has demonstrated that industrial arbitration can be low-key and responsive.

(1) It is the servant of the parties to agreements, and aims to serve their needs;

(2) These needs have grown, as statistics of cases testify;

(3) Deficiencies that are criticised are largely procedural in character, and are being tackled, e.g., in the steel industry by devices such as expedited arbitration;

(4) It is capable of providing constructive solutions to the problems of parties, in the setting of their industrial relations situation;

(5) Arbitration does not equal legalism.

So much for contract interpretation in the USA. One of the most interesting developments in recent years has, however, been a series of new approaches to the resolution of interest disputes. Various experiments have been undertaken in an endeavour to avoid 'deadline bargaining' when contracts reach the end of their stated life. Continuous bargaining has been attempted, with or without the aid of pre-negotiation committees or *ad hoc* study groups. Preventive mediation has made progress, and mediation-arbitration also has its supporters. 'Final offer selection' has also been much discussed in recent years.

The most significant instance of the use of arbitration in interest disputes is the final and binding voluntary arbitration which the steel industry agreed experimentally for its 1974 wage negotiations. While management had to pay a high price for a new agreement, the fact that it was concluded before the previous agreement expired did avoid the classic steel industry problem of stockpiling in advance of new contract negotiations, followed by a rundown of stocks and layoffs after a new agreement had been concluded. New peace-keeping arrangements no doubt have their costs, but they may be cheaper over the long haul. It may be more costly to wait until the industrial house is on fire.

These experimental and innovative techniques may seem rather 'gimmicky'. They should be viewed instead as instances of a search for alternatives to coercive action in industrial relations. For our purpose they suggest that arbitration may have a very important part to play not only in accommodating some dynamic within existing collective agreements but as a useful mechanism for promoting the settlement of new contract issues.

Canadian experience is also instructive. There is a long tradition in Canada of compulsory conciliation of interest disputes, and a stronger peace obligation than that in the USA for interpretation disputes, amounting to a total ban on stoppages in the course of an agreement's life. Every collective agreement must contain a provision for the final settlement, without stoppage of work, by arbitration or otherwise, of all differences between the parties to or employees bound by the collective agreement as to its interpretation and application.

Some years ago a Task Force which reviewed Canadian labour relations recommended that this ban on stoppages during an agreement's term should be partially lifted.[12] It argued that parties to agreements should be free to resort to economic sanctions in disputes relating to the permanent displacement of employees resulting from industrial conversion (technological change) occurring during the life of a collective agreement.

The issue of technological change, and the job security issues it poses, has been a burning one in Canada for many years. The proposal by the Task Force was controversial but, after successive legislative proposals had been drafted, an enactment passed in 1972 did provide a letout from the absolute prohibition of stoppages while agreements are in force. Now the Canada Labour Code provides that an employer bound by a collective agreement who proposes to make a change in technology which is likely to affect the terms and conditions and employment security of a significant number of his workforce covered by the agreement is required to give notice of the change to the bargaining agent (trade union). The union may seek, via the Canada Labour Board, to serve on the employer notice to bargain, for the purpose of revising the existing provisions or concluding new ones aimed at helping the employees to adjust to the effects of changing technology. It is essentially a contract reopening device, with the consequences for the use of economic sanctions that may follow.

How this new legislative requirement will operate remains to be seen. The definition of 'technological change' itself poses problems of interpretation. For our purposes there are, however, two very significant points to draw out of this change in Canadian practice. First, industrial change may be quite dramatic while an agreement is running its course. The parties are not frozen by an agreement into a *status quo* position. This fits with our thesis that the employment relationship continues to develop while agreements are running. Secondly, and more disquietingly for industrial peacekeeping machinery in general and for arbitration in particular, arbitration may not be able to absorb and disperse powerful pressures that build up within an agreement when technological change brings major manpower problems in its train. Put another way, the parties may not be able to narrow their differences sufficiently to provide an arbitrator with a framework. It is salutary to bear this point in mind, for nothing could do greater harm to the cause of arbitration than the assumption that it can necessarily handle explosive situations, such as rapid technological change.

It would be equally dangerous, however, to rush to the opposite extreme, and conclude that arbitration is capable of coping only with *status quo* problems, to be resolved in a retrospective, judicial and narrow interpretative sense. There is a middle ground. The argument of this paper is that there is enough domestic experience, and sufficient instructive testimony from other countries, to encourage us to push forward with arbitration into this middle ground. We end by drawing the following conclusions or 'inferences'.

(1) Arbitration is more than fire-fighting. It can play a fire prevention role, in performing a positive and constructive function in the continuing industrial relations scene.

(2) The terminology of 'rights' and 'interest' applied to disputes may be unhelpful, in that it tends to polarise discussion of appropriate industrial peace-keeping machinery. It may then be easier in Britain than in countries which do draw such a distinction to move in the direction of firmer institutional devices, such as arbitration, for reaching accommodations between the parties to collective bargaining.

(3) It does not follow that when collective agreements are legally enforceable there must be a strong involvement of the law in resolving contract interpretation disputes. North American experience suggests the opposite.

(4) If arbitration is seen as having a constructive and prospective role, and not simply a backward-looking function, the sparse content of many British collective agreements, a matter which caused the Donovan Commission great concern with regard to arbitration as an aid to effective procedures, is not an obstacle to its wider use.

(5) The traditional animus against arbitration, that it has no general governing principles, is rubbish. No such requirement need be made of it. 'Splitting the difference' may often be perfectly sensible and rational.

(6) Equally, the debate as to reasoned awards by arbitrators is a sterile one. On the whole arbitrators are likely to serve the cause of constructive industrial relations better if they do state reasons for their awards. It is a *non sequitur* to equate this with legally or consensually binding 'case law'.

(7) An extended use of arbitration must not allow the parties to abdicate their primary responsibility for industrial self-government. Arbitrators should not be slow to decline jurisdiction and refuse to make awards if they judge that the parties have not themselves made serious endeavours to resolve their differences.

(8) Much more needs to be known about the scale and practice of arbitration in Britain. The prevailing philosophy is that awards are the property of the parties to them. Greater publicity to awards would help to increase the stock of knowledge about arbitration cases. By the same token it would add to the stock of expertise about arbitration.

(9) There is a need for follow-up research on arbitration awards, in order to discover what actually happened to the subsequent industrial relationships following on the implementation of an award.

In recent years there has been a surfeit of posturing in British industrial relations. Arbitration has been utilised on a very modest scale. It is the essence of this paper that it can have a low-key yet constructive role in our industrial relations system. We certainly need more public discussion of its pros and cons, and a meeting of the British Association is surely a most appropriate forum in which to plead for and seek to initiate such a dialogue.

Notes

1. Lord Amulree, *Industrial Arbitration in Great Britain*, London, 1929; Mary T. Rankin, *Arbitration Principles and the Industrial Court*, London, 1931.
2. Amulree, op. cit., p. 183 ff.
3. Otto Kahn-Freund, *Labour and the Law*, London, 1972, pp. 56 ff.
4. K. W. Wedderburn, Conflicts of 'Rights' and Conflicts of 'Interest' in Labour Disputes, in Benjamin Aaron (ed.) *Dispute Settlement Procedures in Five Western Countries*, University of California, 1969.
5. K. W. Wedderburn and P. L. Davies, *Employment Grievances and Disputes Procedures in Britain*, University of California, 1969, p. 160.

G

6. Rankin, op. cit., pp. 9–10.
7. Royal Commission on Trade Unions and Employers' Associations, Minutes of Evidence 45, 26 July 1966. Witness Sir Roy Wilson, QC, President of the Industrial Court, p. 1936.
8. Royal Commission on Trade Unions and Employers' Associations 1965–1968 (Chairman Lord Donovan), *Cmnd. 3623*, London, 1968, p. 73, para 287.
9. Royal Commission, Minutes of Evidence loc. cit., pp. 1934–6.
10. For a recent review of arbitration in the USA see symposium on 'New directions in grievance handling and arbitration' in *Monthly Labor Review*, November 1972, Volume 95, no. 11.
11. R. F. Lythgoe, On improving arbitration: the transcript trauma, *Monthly Labor Review*, June 1974, Volume 97, no. 6, p. 47 *et seq.*
12. *Canadian Industrial Relations*. The Report of the Task Force on Labour Relations, Ottawa, 1969, p. 174, para 596 *et seq.*
    It is important to note that the tide of discussion in Canada is not all flowing against arbitration. For an eloquent statement of the case for arbitration as a responsible alternative to the strike, see Judge Walter Little, The Role of Arbitration in Industrial Relations, keynote address, Industrial Relations Centre, Queen's University at Kingston, Ontario, 1974.

7

Big Business and Big Science

*Harry Townsend**

Derek de Solla Price has familiarised us all with the fact that we live in an era of big science: as many scientists alive today as in the whole of recorded history; scientists, patents, publications and so on all growing exponentially, the literature in the theory of determinants, non-Euclidian geometry, X-rays, and experimental psychology, the number of asteroids known and the number of engineers, all doubling every ten years. We live with a rate of technological change radically different from anything which has gone before.

Similarly the rate of growth in the size of businesses and the concentration of industrial activity is without precedent. The five biggest companies in the United Kingdom, with sales in excess of £10 billion, have 15 per cent of the turnover of the largest 1,000 companies; the fifty largest have 46 per cent of the turnover; the three largest company employers, GEC, British Leyland, and ICI between them employ as many men as are occupied on all our farms; British Petroleum's sales receipts are just about double the rates of revenue of all the local authorities in England and Wales. Just as the output of science has been accelerating over the last generation, so has the concentration of manufacturing industry: in 1958, the 100 largest firms were responsible for 31 per cent of net output in manufacturing; in 1970, for 45 per cent. In 157 product groups for which comparisons can be made, the proportion of sales made by the five largest firms rose from an average of 56 per cent in 1958 to an average of 65 per cent in 1968.

Research and development and the size of firms

Research and development *programmes* are highly concentrated in

* Professor of Economics, University of Lancaster.

all the countries for which statistics are available. For example, in the mid-1960s, the four largest research and development programmes undertaken by individual firms accounted for 26 per cent of research and development work in the UK, the eight largest accounted for 34 per cent, and the twenty largest for 47 per cent. The position was similar in the USA, where the corresponding percentages were 22, 35 and 57, in Sweden with percentages of 33, 43 and 54, and in France with 21, 31 and 48 per cent.[1]

These programmes are mainly performed in firms with more than 5,000 employees. However, the degree of concentration of research and development expenditure is less when firms are ranked by employment than by size of programme. In the USA, for instance, the 200 largest programmes approximately equal the outlays of the 470 largest firms (i.e. firms with more than 5,000 employees), and so it is evident that many large firms cannot be spending a great deal on research and development. Similarly, in France, the 200 largest programmes accounted for 91 per cent of total expenditure, but the 200 largest employers accounted for no more than 72 per cent.

When one concedes this qualification, we are still left with most research and development being undertaken by large firms. Firms employing more than 5,000 employees account for 88 per cent of all industrial research and development in the USA, about 75 per cent in Germany, and about 60 per cent in France. The FBI Survey (1961) suggested that British firms with more than 10,000 employees accounted for nearly 60 per cent of research and development. The vast majority of small firms do not undertake any formal research and development. When the firms, large or small, which perform research and development are examined as a separate group, there is a significant correlation between size of labour force and size of research and development programme in most industries.

So far we have been considering the absolute size of research activity; but the relative extent of such activity, research per man or, as it is most usually measured, research per £1 of net sales, may also be important. If you think of two firms, one with sales of 300 and the other with sales of 100, with the larger devoting 1 per cent of sales to research and the smaller devoting 2 per cent of sales to research, then the larger would have a programme 50 per cent greater although its research intensity were only half as great. The evidence about research intensity is ambiguous. There is much weaker correlation between research intensity and size of firm than between research expenditure and size of firm. It is not significant in many industries, and in a few industries in both Europe and the USA smaller firms show higher research intensities. Among the larger firms there is some evidence that research intensity diminishes with size above a certain level, e.g. that research and development as a percentage of sales falls when sales exceed £150–200m.

This last finding is subject to a number of interpretations. If there are economies of scale in research and development, research expenditure should fall as a percentage of sales as a firm's sales rise. On the other hand, if the monopoly power of a firm increases with its sales, then it might find itself protected from the need to engage in proportionately as much expenditure as in more competitive circumstances.,

Advantages of big business

One cannot settle an argument simply by listing advantages and disadvantages: the completeness of each list can always be questioned and the weight as well as kind of advantage needs to be assessed. Nevertheless, it is much easier to discover advantages than disadvantages. I will mention four of them.

First, industrial research and development is a recent example of the division of labour, specialisation in work which only becomes profitable as the scale of activity grows. This specialisation stems partly from the growing complexity of technology in such fields as chemicals and electronics which makes a higher education essential before anyone can have the minimum qualification for innovation. Specialised research and development is also required in chemicals, and in other fields, where flow of production has replaced batch production. When goods are produced one at a time a new method or modification in design can be tried out in the plant; but with flow lines experiment in the plant becomes prohibitively expensive. It also becomes technically inefficient compared with equipping specialised research workers with specialised equipment.

Discussion of these points is often obscured by the romantic examples that are often quoted of virtuoso performances by inventors. These deserve every credit, but important invention is not what industrial innovation is mostly about: most of the time the effort is devoted to development rather than fundamental research, to the further application of known techniques or the further improvement of existing products or processes. In this mundane work advantage lies with the well-equipped industrial laboratory rather than with the individual inventor. Christopher Freeman illustrates this point from the plastics industry, where of 4,239 patents taken out between 1791 and 1930, 43 per cent were taken out by individuals and 57 per cent by firms; of 5,132 patents taken out between 1931 and 1945, 15 per cent were for individuals and 85 per cent for firms; and of 6,238 patents taken out between 1946 and 1955, 8 per cent were for individuals and 92 per cent for firms.

A second advantage is found in another conventional source of economies of scale: indivisibilities. These occur in research and development in the form of thresholds that must be crossed before projects can be successfully undertaken. A rough rule of thumb would be that, outside the aerospace industry, the average annual cost per qualified scientist is £20,000. A minimum team of 5 scientists would therefore cost £100,000. If 2 per cent of turnover is considered a reasonable figure for research and development total sales of £5m, the output of about 1,500 workers would be required for a minimum research team. Small firms cannot normally join in the game.

This point is reinforced in industries where development expenditures have to be made to satisfy regulatory bodies. For example, it costs about £750,000 to carry out the tests required by the US Government before a new ethical drug can be marketed. Only a large company could undertake such expenditure, which no amount of pharmacological genius can reduce in size. The same effect may be seen on a very much greater scale in the case of the testing of new aircraft and the demonstration of air-worthiness.

Such large indivisible items of expenditure represent one kind of financial hazard which is typical of the research and development area. Research by its nature is a journey into the unknown and as such is one of the riskier industrial activities. Managers may easily underestimate costs, time and manpower required, and overestimate the probability of technical success, market acceptance, market life and prospective revenue. In these circumstances, large financial resources become a prerequisite for long-term success, and constitute the third advantage of large firms. It is perhaps appropriate in a part of the country where the Kirk is strong to recall the principle of 'gamblers' ruin'. Even when the chances of success are quite high it is possible to lose one's shirt just by a normal run of bad luck. For example, if a series of gambles have a 1 in 5 chance of success, then there is an 80 per cent chance of losing a first bet. The chance of doing this twice in succession is $0.8 \times 0.8 = 0.64$, i.e. 64 per cent chance. There is a 51 per cent chance of losing three times in succession, and a 33 per cent chance of losing 5 times in a row. In order to reduce the risk of losing below 10 per cent, eleven bets would have to be laid. In firms where radical research is attempted, e.g. to develop a new therapeutic principle, a continuous run of bad luck is always possible. In more mundane areas the picture is not o black because the risk of failure should normally be reduced as he research progresses. Bets need not be laid in full before the beginning of the race. As the research proceeds its prospects become clearer, success can be reinforced, failure can be cut out. However, at this stage a subjective risk, also familiar to gamblers, intrudes. If a lot of money has been spent on a project which always held out promise it is difficult to acknowledge failure and cut the losses. (The Concorde Catch', if you wish.)

Large firms can bear risks more successfully than small firms by spreading their investment over a range of projects. They can also gain by being able to finance parallel approaches to individual projects. This advantage has been demonstrated in the United States where it has been possible to try multiple solutions to reactor designs whereas in Britain we have had to concentrate on single solutions. The same advantage has been seen in the US aerospace industry. So long as the value of information gained from pursuing several alternatives exceeds the additional cost, the larger research programme will be economically more efficient.

The fourth advantage of large firms lies in the scale of their ordinary production activities: the larger the rate of output the smaller will any development cost be per unit of output, as any aircraft manufacturer will tell. Similarly the discovery of improved methods which reduce costs will yield greater return the larger the output for which they may be used. And if scale of production is the reward for efficiency, this efficiency may contribute to the speed with which new methods or products can be introduced. Research and development may thus be better suited to large firms as well as large firms suited to research and development.

However, all is not on the side of the big battalions. Those who think small is beautiful could urge at least two arguments against the suitability of large firms for innovation.

Disadvantages of big business

One has to remember that when speaking of firms one is not referring to single, tightly jointed entities, but to organisations made up of men and women. As the firm gets larger the organisations inevitably becomes more bureaucratic and hierarchical.

Bureaucracies have harboured men of imagination and vision but a formal organisation is liable to set a low value on such qualities. The smooth running of an administration depends upon order and order is most readily achieved by continuing to do the same things from day to day. If innovation has to be assimilated the tendency

96   HARRY TOWNSEND

may well be to over-organise the change and so to make it unnecessarily costly.

The effects of bureaucracies striving for order are compounded as
they grow in size by the fact that they must usually grow more
hierarchical. Hierarchies have qualities of their own. At the
simplest they constitute a series of sieves through which proposals
must be filtered as they pass to decision-making levels. This may
make for better decisions as different amounts of experience and
kinds of expertise are brought to bear, but it may also make for
negative decisions. Hierarchies are also career structures and wrong
decisions put careers and reputations at risk. One of the striking
features of hierarchical organisations is the length of their collective
memory, especially for mistakes. This is partly because records are
kept, but mostly because it is in many people's interest to remember. As mistakes carry a lasting penalty, and mistakes of commission
are much more readily identified than mistakes of omission, the
chances that someone will say 'No' to a proposal for change
increase as the size of the hierarchy grows.

These disadvantages of size are real but they are not insur-
mountable. The oil companies that are operating at the limits of
technological knowledge in the deep waters off Scotland are
bureaucratic and hierarchical in all conscience, but they have found
ways of creating and using a whole range of new techniques.

We can sum up the relationship between size of firms and their
suitability for science-based innovation in a series of propositions
about the comparative advantages of large and small firms. Large
firms have advantages in the deployment of resources for organised
research, in coping with the indivisibilities and risks of innovation,
and in enjoying the fruits of research over large outputs; but the
weight of advantage may lie with smaller organisations so far as
the motivation for change is concerned, the willingness to face
uncertainty and the flexibility to adopt new products or new
technologies.

Growth in the size of manufacturing firms has meant not simply
firms with greater outputs but also firms with greater proportions
of the total output of individual products. The question therefore
arises as to whether competition or monopoly is more conducive to
innovation.

Research, Development and Concentration

Evidence on the relationship between innovation and concentration
is ambiguous and is mainly confined to the United States. This has

not prevented commentators from taking up firm positions. The most influential has probably been J. A. Schumpeter who wrote 'What we have got to accept is that [the large-scale establishment or unit of control] has come to be the most powerful engine of [economic] progress. ... In this respect perfect competition is not only impossible but inferior.'[3] J. K. Galbraith has echoed this view very loudly.

The Schumpeter/Galbraith view is partly based on the advantages of large firms for innovation; but limitations on competition introduce some additional considerations. First, the prospect of gaining a monopoly profit by being the first with an innovation provides an incentive to innovate. This has been a traditional argument in favour of the patent system, but a special profit may be available to the innovator whether a change is patentable or not.

Monopoly profit may provide an incentive to innovate but it can be argued that this incentive is only likely to be effective when it is the prospect of a new monopoly position which is in question; an established monopoly may have it so good that it has little motive to disturb its pleasant situation. However, this argument has now been stood on its head by economists who have identified established monopoly positions with the existence of financial and organisational slack—resources used for excess reserves and managerial purposes. One of these purposes may be the pursuit of technological advance out of technological interest, a pursuit dear to production managers. The quiet life which some have seen as the reward for monopoly need not be one of scientific tranquility.

There is another element of incentive which may come into play when production is concentrated. The gain from an innovation may be external to a firm making the change. This could be the case where a competitive firm discovers a non-patentable way of reducing costs, e.g. by introducing a reorganisation of clerical work. Competitors will copy the new method and the gain will be competed away in lower prices to customers. A monopolist would internalise this external gain and so would have a greater incentive to make the change.

Irrespective of the lure of further monopoly profit as a spur to research and development, there is the fact that the existence of profits will provide the wherewithal for research. Research and development are by their nature only suited to finance from retained profits (or by taxpayers). Money cannot normally be borrowed or raised on equity terms for research and development because there is no tangible asset to provide security for creditors or definable prospect for ordinary shareholders. Rolls-Royce showed that equity capital can be raised for research and development, but they could scarcely have provided a more compelling demonstration of the dangers involved.

Finally, there is the argument that when the number of competitors is limited price competition is likely to be muted; but that when competition is restrained in one direction it is likely to be released in other directions. Competition in innovation may take the place of price competition. There is probably a good deal in this argument as any competitor can match a price cut but only equally skilful competitors can match improved processes and new products. Oligopoly and innovation may go together, as they do, for

Figure 1

*Ranking of the top 10 companies in the UK market
for prescription medicines*

1962   1970

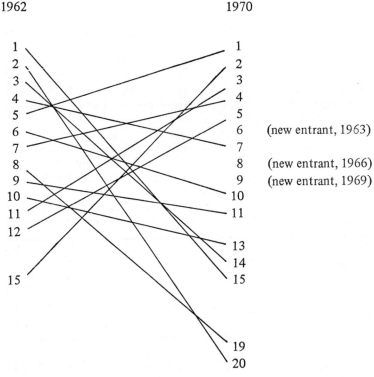

Source: NEDO, Chemicals EDC, *Focus on Pharmaceuticals*, HMSO 1972,
    Appendix A.

example, in the pharmaceutical industry. This may be seen in the changing rank order of the top compainies where positions change with the success of their products rather than with the cuts (although these happen) in their prices.

Part of the difficulty of establishing the connection between monopoly, competition and innovation turns on the usage of words. Restricted competition to some observers means some kinds of market structure, e.g. oligpoly; to other observers it means activity aimed at getting ahead of a rival. Active competition in the latter sense may take place in market structures that the theorist would label 'monopolistic'. When this is recognised the association between industrial concentration and research and development may seem as natural to advocates of competition as to apologists for monopoly.

Notes

1. I had the good fortune to edit the book by Christopher Freeman, *Economics of Industrial Innovation*, which is soon to be published in the Penguin Modern Economic series, and I have relied on this authoritative work for much of the evidence in this section.
2. C. Freeman's source is J. Delorme, *Anthologie des Brevets sur les Matieres Plastiques* (3 vols.), Amphora, 1962.
3. J. A. Schumpeter, *Capitalism, Socialism and Democracy*, p. 106.

8

Managing Change

*R. Scholey**

This paper deals with the management of change, making particular reference to the converging streams of technical and social changes affecting the steel industry. The industry, itself, is very much the progeny of change: change brought about by the massive events of the Industrial Revolution in the nineteenth century.

At the beginning of this century, such iron and steel as was produced, was made very much on the 'cottage' industry basis, drawing on forests for the manufacture of charcoal, and water power from the rivers for driving forging hammers, or, as they were known in those days, 'tilt' hammers, made principally from wooden beams. The exploitation of coal, and its application for steam-raising, changed much of this, and so towards the end of the nineteenth century, iron and steel were made primarily in works, the largest of which would employ a few thousand people, sited near coal fields and iron-ore deposits.

We could, perhaps, pause here and consider the foundation of the Industrial Revolution in this country, a major cornerstone of which was iron and steelmaking. Steelmaking centres grew up where coal and iron-ore were locally available, and both quantity and quality were ample for the needs of that time. Transport was relatively undeveloped and such overseas deposits or iron-ore that were known at the time would have proved uneconomic compared with the plentiful home ores. The leading part that Britain played in world affairs up to 1914 enabled the industry to operate vigorously and employ, by the standards of those days, the most advanced technical equipment.

I will not make lengthy reference to the social problems of the day, involving the migration of people from rural areas to the towns to become wage earners in such industry. Although, interest-

* Chief Executive and Board Member, British Steel Corporation.

ingly enough, evidence of such migration still exists today. One, of which I have knowledge, is when Lysaghts moved their works from Wolverhampton to Newport, and the work people migrated with the factory, and lived out in the open while the new plant was being assembled at Newport. Today, the streets in which the works people eventually lived are named after districts of Wolverhampton, although, now, the whole area is submerged in the Welsh way of life.

Following the First World War, as we all know, we entered into a period of extreme economic and industrial disturbance up to the early thirties, during which time unemployment and depression prevailed. Technology went through few advances, and there were halting attempts to rationalise the industry behind a protective tariff wall.

The Second World War saw a resurgence of activity, mainly with equipment which was, by this time, outmoded. Technical developments coming into view included the fully continuous strip mill and the fully continuous billet mill, neither of which were prominently in evidence in Britain. Ironmaking was, basically, dependent on high phosphorous lead, home ore deposits, and steel-making dependent on the open hearth furnace, which was mainly fuelled by coal.

It is from the end of the Second World War that some of the main features of change commenced.

The political consequences of the war were that many countries which, hitherto, had been dependent on Western Europe and the United States' steel supplies, started to develop their own raw material resources of oil, and ore and coal deposits, to effect the first stirrings of national virility by building steel plants of their own. This tended to erode the traditional markets of the established steel producing countries. At home, the by-product of affluence resulted in increasingly more expensive labour, thereby stimulating management to less manpower intensive plant and layouts. Many of the technical spin-offs from the Second World War, in the form of computers, and sophisticated control equipment, reduced the dependency on human skills for production techniques; while the trend to fully continuous production lines, in place of the older, manually-operated practices, speeded up.

Rising above this was the advent of low cost, bulk tonnage oxygen, and the development at 'Linz Donawitz' of the first large basic oxygen furnace, which was ultimately to produce up to 300 tonnes of steel in a sixth of the time that the old open hearth furnaces could produce 100 tonnes, with great reductions in manpower. To this list, one might add the need for richer ores and the development of large, bulk-carrying ocean vessels, which were capable of transporting coal and ore at low cost to Europe from the rich deposits that had been opened up overseas.

Even before nationalisation, the effect of all these factors was beginning to impinge markedly on the iron and steel industry. I suppose one of the first places in which this took place in Britain was at Port Talbot, where a new strip mill was put down in 1952, together with a new open hearth shop, which was the largest in Europe. Concurrently with this, there was a rationalisation of the traditional Welsh tinplate Industry, which had been based on over 20 small units spread over a large area of Wales, into two large units at Trostre and Velindre, near to the Port Talbot works.

Here was a clear instance of technology impinging on a large regional social scene. These small units employed about 6,000 people and were widely dispersed. Trostre and Velindre now employ about 4,000 people. The whole operation was carried out extremely smoothly, with tremendous co-operation between the trade unions and the management of the Steel Company of Wales. Within fifteen years, the advance of technology meant that the open hearth furnace could no longer compete with the BOS process, and a new two vessel BOS plant—fed from a new deepwater harbour—replaced all the open hearths at Port Talbot in 1970. Again, there was tremendous co-operation in minimising the social problem caused by manpower reduction.

Meanwhile, nearby at Llanwern, a new strip mill had been constructed, which was commissioned in 1961, based on BOF, and designed very much to replace the ageing equipment at Ebbw Vale. This, in the event, did not happen, which left Ebbw Vale withering on the bough, to the extent that it still remains a problem today.

This was a period during which, in spite of the British Iron and Steel Federation's co-ordinating activities, new development nevertheless, proceeded, in a somewhat haphazard and conflicting way.

Whatever we may, or may not, think about the nationalisation of iron and steel, it did in the event afford an opportunity to draw together all the threads of advancing technology into a coherent development plan, in such a way that would not have been possible under the old company structure. By so doing, it emphasised the problems of social implication which, coincidentally, have raised public comment concerning the effects of largeness, bureaucracy, and the impersonalisation and institutionalisation of the effects of large industry.

If, then, we first consider the technical implications, the fact is that, in the main, the steel industry throughout the world has turned towards deepwater ports, to foreign imported ore, to BOF practice, to automated means of production and materials handling. This has meant that new developments are best sited on the coast, in many cases distant from the traditional centres of production—this is, the old coalfields of Wales, Staffordshire, the Rhur and Alsace—leaving behind communities which were virtually one hundred per cent dependent for their livelihoods on iron, steel and coal.

Clearly, solutions have to be found. What is glaringly apparent is that there is a reluctance for communities to move to new areas of work—rather, new work has to be brought to the communities, requiring all the efforts of industry and government, both local and national, to effect this in such a way that it can be sensibly phased-in with the technical changes I have described.

The machinery adopted by the Corporation has been roughly along the following lines.

At works level, particular attention is given to point consultative methods in order to ensure that personnel, at all levels, are made aware of the implications of, and the reasons for, technical change or the exploitation of economies of scale, within the industry. The importance of discussing the social implications arising from techno-logical innovations cannot be over-emphasised, particularly as the successful introduction of these changes largely depends on the continued co-operation of employees and their unions. Notice of plant closures has been given as far in advance as possible—some-times over two years, so that plans can be fully formulated.

The first consideration must be the effective redeployment, where possible, of employees affected by changes in their working prac-tices or environment, or, in some cases, the total disappearance of their job or activity, with the aim of minimising redundancy as far as is practicable.

In order to reduce the impact of any impending change, a counselling service has been developed to help individuals consider the alternative opportunities available to them. Employee participa-tion is encouraged and a counselling team may be made up of individuals from a wide variety of backgrounds, including trade union representatives. At the final stage of counselling, close co-operation is maintained with the Employment Services Agency to ensure the successful placement of employees in new jobs.

For those who cannot be redeployed immediately, with their existing skills, a training and re-training scheme has been introduced to enable them to switch to new jobs, whether within the Corpora-tion or elsewhere. Finally, in those areas where employment opportunities have had to be reduced as a result of technological developments, every effort has been made to attract new industries to the areas, in co-operation with the appropriate Development Councils.

At the heart of the problem is our old friend 'communications': how to get across to the work force, their families and the local community, the need for change. To make them aware of the fact that if we are to survive, we cannot do so with outmoded machinery and uneconomic techniques. The fact that in order to operate competitively with rival commodities at home, and with other steel producing concerns abroad, we need men with new skills in the right areas—as has so often been the case in the past during periods of large-scale industrial change.

It might almost be said that, in order to protect 200,000 jobs we have to lose 50,000 job opportunities; but we must do our utmost to ensure that our purpose is fully understood. Of course, it would be foolish to think that such changes in a community are made without the generation of great emotive forces, and it is here that the consultative skills have to play their part.

My own feeling is that the development of joint consultation is not adequate to take the full force of the strains which are being imposed on us at the present time. Within the steel industry, attitudes vary, reflecting very much the differences of old companies: some companies were pioneering consultative fields as early as 1930. Today, however, we are in a position where the full cost-operating facts, prices, constitution of order books, are available to our work force, and we train our work people to understand the interpretation of the figures in exactly the same manner as our management would. This is the only way to create a confidence, a 'lingua franca' whereby meaningful discussions can be held which will enable progress to be made towards resolving the human problems surrounding technical change.

When new equipment is being contemplated, whether large or small, the work force should be informed at the conceptual stage; they should be taken through the commercial reasons for the implications in respect of cost and manning; if necessary they should be given an opportunity to see what is involved themselves—and, certainly before the equipment comes into being at the works, there should be an adequate training programme prepared in which they are both consulted and involved.

I suppose that in all this, without appearing to state the obvious, the two main agencies involved are the management and the trade unions.

All too frequently we read and hear complaints about the lack of effectiveness of the trade union establishment, as opposed to the power of 'grass roots' force, and this is something which requires, and receives, considerable time and attention today. In no situation are these relationships tested to their utmost more than in that relating to industrial change of the kind I have been describing. I believe that we, in the steel industry, have a vested interest in restoring the effectiveness of the trade union establishment in respect of the affairs of its members.

During the course of our recently announced development programme, involving numerous closures, we have been involved with all sorts of pressure groups, action committees and the like, who have been opposing us in what one might call an 'uncontrolled' or 'undirected' way. This phenomenon is not new. Most people are resistant to change, and similar reactions have been experienced in the past wherever communities have been affected in this way. I believe that much of this reaction stems from the sense of shock which work people have felt when they find their particular situation under threat. This could be avoided if, over the years, meaningful consultation in depth were undertaken by management, to put across to work people the strengths and weaknesses of their situations against the march of advancing technology.

It is certainly my experience that when people have been given time, and by that I mean years, to digest the economic factors surrounding their situation they accept these with far less distress because, obviously, it gives them time to adjust their own personal circumstances accordingly—either by moving into new jobs or by helping management to arrive at alternative solutions to what seems to be an inevitable trend.

This paper opened with a reference to the converging streams of technical and social change affecting the steel industry, both of which I have now briefly described. I would like to end by discussing the pressures these two streams exercise on management.

It is sometimes said that industrial management inclines to technical change, finding technical problems challenging and more responsive to solution than those relating to the human, social, side. This, of course, may have some substance. We must, however, recognise that management itself is also the subject of change at the same time. Not only have its loyalties been disturbed, as I mentioned previously, but it is also confronted with many other problems.

First, there has been the progressive weakening of the general authority and paternalistic attitudes of management, which were to be found in some parts of the iron and steel industry. I should say that, in many ways, the iron and steel industry has been an extremely conservative industry, and has tried to preserve many of the old traditional links between manager and work force. But the personal qualities required to deal with the demands of the present industrial scene require more thought and subsequent re-training. Re-training

H

an older manager is not always easy, while younger management potential can consider the problems so daunting that they seek their fortunes elsewhere than in an industry which involves them in shift-work in the early stages.

The trend towards unionisation of staff, particularly in the lower and middle management areas, has been one modification which has caused a degree of bewilderment: foremen and middle management no longer act as effectively as they used to, as the 'sergeant majors' of the industry. They have, on the way, lost a degree of automatic protection, both in terms of wages and conditions, while at the same time senior management pressure is coming more to bear on the way they discharge their duties. And with nationalisation, new and universal management codes for the industry have been evolved, which result in changes of status, attitude to job, and conditions.

This paper has been largely concerned with 'the growth of size'. Size breeds impersonality, impersonality affects management as much as it affects work grades. I defy anyone to find the man who does not like to feel that he is known as an individual within the organisation for which he works—and by known, I mean, known at the top. This, of course, becomes particularly difficult with the growth of large organisations such as ours, and although one can counter the effects of size (as far as management is concerned) by such institutional techniques as 'management development assessment schemes', etc., there is still no substitute for personal contact. This requires enormous effort on the part of those at the top, together with a degree of elapsed time.

Much has yet to be done in respect of the management of size. In my own view, it is no use thinking that the advent of size, together with its ensuing problems, can be managed using worn-out techniques. All the forces of rapid communication and transport, together with the harnessing of individual effort in pursuit of common policies, need to be deployed if we are to succeed. I feel in particular that we must break the management of the large works down into units of approximately 2,000 men; such units being encouraged to develop a feeling of entity and belonging. This sounds easier to achieve than it might prove in practice.

I would like to conclude, therefore, by suggesting that the 'twin-streams' of technical and social change cannot be either coped with, or harnessed, without the existence of a stabilised management force, which has confidence in itself, in its superiors, and which is encouraged to deploy all its native initiative and intellect and imagination. Size can be created conceptually, at a stroke; but time and training is needed to overcome its concomitant problems.

Change in the Scottish Context

9

The Political Economy of Change

*K. J. W. Alexander**

The title 'political economy of change' directs attention to all forms
of change, but with an emphasis on the economic and an attempt
to emphasise, by the use of the term 'political economy', the need
for an approach somewhat broader than that usually adopted by
economists.

The meaning usually given to political economy has its origins
in the work of the Scottish moralists of the eighteenth century. Hume
in his *Essays on Commerce* (1752) relates the study of commerce
and of wealth to their effect on the power of the State as well as on
the happiness of individuals. Adam Smith in the *Wealth of Nations*
(1776) took a somewhat narrower view, as he indicated by the comment that the Physiocrats 'treat not only of what is properly called
Political Economy, or of the nature and causes of the Wealth of
Nations, but of every other branch of the system of civil government'.[1] In so narrowing the range of economic inquiry—in opposition to Hume and to the other Scottish moralists who were much
more 'sociological' in their approach—Smith prepared the way for
the development of a more precise and analytical approach to the
study of economics, to which the status of the subject and the
contribution it has made to human welfare owe much. It is also true,
however, that the exclusion of governmental and sociological influences tended to be applied more rigorously as time went on. This
was in part a reflection of the search for scientific objectivity, in
part the attraction of analytical clarity and in part the inevitable
schismatic tendencies of a developing specialism. Unfortunately for
economics the exclusion of these so called 'impurities' and frictions
has increased as their impact on the subject matter of economics

* Professor of Economics, Strathclyde University. This paper is a
shortened version of the Section 'F' (Economics) Presidential Address
at the 1974 Meeting of the British Association, first published in the
January 1975 number of *The Political Quarterly*.

has increased. Government intervention in economic policy, the growth of trade unionism and the development of collective bargaining are the most obvious of a range of illustrations which could be offered to support this contention. Writing in 1932 Lord Robbins suggested that the approach which regarded 'the subject matter of economics as something social and collective' had become 'less and less convenient'.[2] This view was in error then, and experience since has demonstrated the error even more conclusively. Indeed without to any extent qualifying his preference for liberalism over collectivism Lord Robbins has more recently[3] put much greater emphasis on the relationship between the social, political and economic factors. My use of the term political economy strays from the narrow path of Smithian virtue and is closer to that of Hume, of Ferguson and of Dugald Stewart, dealing with the mechanics of decision-taking, with administrative processes and with the objectives of choice, that is with ends affected by values. This is a much broader approach than that adopted by most modern economists who focus attention on the calculus of choice rather than on its mechanics, and who try to exclude judgements affecting the objectives of choice.

An economist describing the conditions best suited to bring about economic change would find it difficult to exclude from his work all concern for the sociological consequences of particular changes. An economist who is not describing but prescribing conditions for change is—either implicitly or explicitly—embodying some non-economic components of change in the economic goals he has adopted. He could wash his hands of such broader policy implications by arguing that they are unprovable, falling back on the Scottish moralists' enigma of unintended social outcomes: 'nations stumble upon establishments, which are indeed the result of human action, but not the execution of any human design'.[4] But this would underestimate the development of the social sciences in the two hundred years since Ferguson expressed that view. Lord Robbins concludes his essay *On the Relations between Politics and Economics* with a rhetorical question which comes near to adopting the opposite view:

> ... must we not also contend that science—social science, the product of mind reflecting upon itself and the social universe about it—for good or for bad, can change the world and as our examples (Smith, Marx, Keynes) show, has indeed sometimes done so.[5]

Increasingly economics is linked with policy, implying action which is conscious in intent and collective in nature.

All economic commentaries on change place considerable emphasis upon investment, some of which will be in the public sector and be financed partly from fiscal sources. Implicitly if not explicitly the notion of social time preference has been introduced. The balance aimed for between investment in public and private goods has a major influence on a society's characteristics. More specifically the extent to which a society intends that the provision of infrastructure—roads, houses, etc.—shall precede economic development (as a way of inducing it, e.g. in a less developed region and as an element in economic planning) or, in contrast, respond to it (as in the industrial development of Britain in the nineteenth century) will greatly influence the 'quality of life' not only during the period of rapid development but for several decades thereafter. Most pointedly of all, decisions about investment in human beings, in the form of education, training and re-training for change, will affect the pace and character of the change which occurs, and not only of the economic change but of the social and political changes which are associated with it. Prescribing for economic change has implications for other aspects of life which are too closely related to economic change to allow the economist to enjoy the freedom from responsibility for them which he might wish and which he sometimes lays claim to. Economic development has implications for the structure of industry, and for the relationship of the individual to the productive process and to the structure of authority. Any policy for economic development (or change) will have specific outcomes affecting the individual not only as consumer but as employee. The economist cannot exempt himself from problems of alienation and bureaucracy when these are inseparable from a structure of industry determined by his policy for economic development and for the choice of techniques, a key element in any such policy. Policies on the allocation of investment and the structure of industry also relate directly to the relationship between the private and public sectors of an economy, both in terms of their sizes and the influences exercised from each sector on the other. Yet the disciplines of economics, politics and sociology have moved further apart in the groves of academe while in practise their areas of interest have moved closer together and considerably overlapped.

A particularly glaring gap is found in the studies of wage determination by collective bargaining. The majority of recent texts either ignore the crucial concept of bargaining power or use the term without any serious attempt at definition or analysis. Survey articles and books on 'recent trends' or 'comparative studies' in industrial relations similarly ignore the concept completely. Even the case studies of particular disputes which have become fashionable include no analysis of the distribution of bargaining power in the particular situation being described. Such neglect is also a feature of policy oriented writing, by academics and others. Clegg tells us *How to Run an Incomes Policy*[6] without discussing bargaining power. You may comb the reports of the National Board for Prices and Incomes for references, far less treatment, but without success. Arbitrators are perhaps understandably coy about referring to bargaining power, for fear of appearing to endorse their job description of 'awarding the lion's share to the lion'. Certainly in the Wilberforce report[7] there is no discussion of power being exercised beyond the doors of the room in which the hearing took place. In the run-up to the 1974 miners' strike this lacuna was filled by Michael McGahey's slogan 'It wasn't Wilberforce that won us the victory in 1972 but picket force'.

Most power in industrial relations derives from economic factors and is ultimately reflected in market conditions. However the desire to achieve non-economic ends—to save face, to maintain credibility, even to win an election—can affect the behaviour of the parties and produce results which do not derive from economic factors or market conditions. Circumstances which can leave market price indeterminate have received much attention. Trade union organisation and collective bargaining have been accorded the possibility of raising wages because of the existence of 'indeterminacy'. In all such cases there *is* a price or wage and it *has* been determined. It is the theory which is indeterminate, and solutions are only made more difficult by confusing theoretical inadequacy with real world phenomena.

A frequently expressed view is that bargaining power should be equalised (or eliminated?) by a policy combining, possibly, fiscal, administrative and legal measures. Thorough exploration of such a proposal would take us into the economists' theory of 'the second best' and the objections to piecemeal welfare economics of the kind suggested. It is perhaps enough to assert that lack of precision of the concept of bargaining power and the total absence of measurement or of attempts to measure it, make proposals for equalising it premature even if they could be supported on welfare grounds.

The concept of bargaining power must take account of political as well as of economic factors. The impact of government on bargaining power can be direct, as when it reflects third party interests and attempts to influence the outcome of a particular bargaining situation, or indirect when some policy adopted by government causes a shift in the balance of advantage between the two parties. The indirect influence may be intentional, as Keynes saw the relationship between monetary policy and the miners:

They represent in the flesh the 'fundamental adjustments' engineered by the Treasury and the Bank of England to satisfy the impatience of the City to bridge the 'moderate gap' between $4·40 and $4·86. They (and others to follow) are the 'moderate sacrifice' still necessary to ensure the stability of the gold standard.[8]

In other cases the impact of government on bargaining strength will be an unintended by-product of a policy with quite different intentions. Perhaps the effect of Regional Employment Premium on wages in Scotland may be taken as an empirical example, even although economic theory was used to assure the policy makers that very little of the premium would 'trickle down' to wages. Such economic theory did not allow for the power of coercive comparisons, long frustrated, or for the determination of the Scottish members of UK trade unions to escape the jibe of 'tartan coolies' which had been fraternally made to them by their better paid colleagues in the English Midlands. Of course the most notable bargaining by-product of politics comes in the field of employment policy: '... if by now it is widely accepted that the maintenance of full employment is a precondition of gaining and retaining political power, then the voting power of the "post-Keynesian" wage earner is a political resource that indirectly affects his bargaining power in the labour market'.[9] In the now highly politicised field of wage determination it would be difficult for anyone to argue that economic analysis alone provides an adequate guide to understanding wage structures and wage movements. Yet economists continue to teach and write as though it does. The shift to political economy is nowhere more necessary if economists are to contribute to the development of changed ways of determining incomes which will be free from the leap-frogging lunacies and inflationary injustices which can and do arise from our present ways.

One of the most widely applied techniques developed by economists is cost-benefit analysis which attempts to embrace considerations beyond the narrowly economic and have them taken account of in decision-taking. It is interesting that the most effective criticism that is made by economists of this technique is that it has an inadequate theoretical basis. This criticism may be turned on its head to say that it would have been impossible to evolve the techniques on the basis of rigorous abstraction and exclusive assumptions of the type favoured by economists. Social sterility may be too high a price to pay for theoretical probity and analytical purity, however, and in this case policy-oriented economists have been unwilling to pay that price. A further weakness of cost-benefit analysis is that data required, particularly for the non-economic elements, is frequently not available, either because it has not been collected or because the elements are difficult or impossible to quantify. Many of these difficulties can be overcome without too great violence being done to common sense, certainly no more than is perpetrated by the most theoretically virtuous of econometricians in his choice of a proxy for some economic variable for which data is lacking. If many of these data difficulties were overcome cost-benefit studies would still face a formidable difficulty, however: the pointers they produce may not have the direction preferred by the decision-takers. Managers and politicians now enjoying the freedom of decision-taking in the absence of a calculus of costs and benefits can, within limits, indulge their own preferences for regions, for votes, for prestige and so on. The curtailment of such freedom will be resisted. It is not surprising that the most far reaching applications of cost-benefit analysis take place where there is an extraneous party who makes aid for a given purpose conditional upon its costs and benefits satisfying rigorous scrutiny. It is because of this that the most thorough exposition of the techniques of cost-benefit are produced for agencies concerned with aid to developing economies, even although the sums being invested and the sophistication required for a sound decision both fall far short of their equivalents in the developed, donor, countries. This point was brought home to me very powerfully when I was involved in a cost-benefit study of a proposed investment in shipbuilding facilities in India. The catalogue of information required far exceeded that on which the decision to establish and finance Upper Clyde Shipbuilders had been taken.

Thus the coming together of economics and politics, the development of an effective political economy, would require not only initiative and change on the part of economists but receptivity and a willingness to change on the part of politicians, and it will be argued shortly that there should be no unconditional surrender by politicians of their freedom to take decisions.

So far most of the change I have discussed is change in political economy rather than change in society on which political economists can usefully comment. Now we concentrate our attention on society undergoing change. Some comments on the Scottish situation will be followed by a few thoughts on change and development in industrial society.

In economic terms Scotland may be regarded as a region of the UK economy. More accurately it could be regarded as three economic regions, the central belt with very strong ties to the rest of the UK economy, the Tayside-Grampian region (Dundee-Aberdeen and their hinterlands) with very strong ties both to the Scottish central belt and to the rest of the UK economy, but rather more export oriented and now the in-shore base for the exploitation of off-shore North Sea oil, and lastly the Highland region with a distinctive economic life but still with important ties to the rest of Scotland and the UK, some oil-related activity and important export-ties (whisky, tourism). Generalisations about 'the Scottish economy' should not lose sight of these distinctions which are themselves very broad-brush and blur finer distinctions of some importance.

Within Scotland the main economic problems have been in West Central Scotland and in the Highlands. What follows concentrates

Table 1

Inter-regional comparisons by key economic indicators

REGION	UNEMPLOYMENT Average monthly rate (males and females combined)			NET MIGRATION 1951–69 as a percentage of population in	EMPLOYMENT CHANGE	
	1971 (%)	1972 (%)	1973 (%)	1951 (%)	1959–68 (%)	1968–71 (%)
West Central Scotland	7·0	7·9	5·7	−13·8	−1·0	−6·4
Scotland	6·0	6·4	4·7	−11·3	+0·6	−3·3
Northern England	5·9	6·3	4·8	−4·2	−0·8	−1·0
Northern Ireland	8·0	8·1	6·3	−11·1	+9·0	+0·4
Wales	4·7	4·9	3·8	−1·9	+2·8	−2·0
Yorkshire & Humberside	4·0	4·2	2·9	−3·1	+4·2*	−3·9
North West England	4·1	4·8	3·6	−3·1	−0·1	−4·1
Merseyside Dev. Area	5·2	7·1	6·0		+6·5	−7·4
W. C. Scotland Special Dev. Area	7·1	8·4	5·9			
Wales S. D. A.	5·6	6·8	4·3			
Northern England S. D. A.	6·8	7·8	5·7			
United Kingdom	3·7	3·8	2·7		+5·2	−2·7

* *includes East Midlands*

Source: West Central Scotland—A Programme of Action.

first on West Central Scotland because it provides an acute illustration of *industrial* difficulty, and is now recognised as having the most
severe problem of any industrial area in Western Europe. Recent
studies of the area's problems have highlighted its poor performance, and Table 1 summarises the situation (see p. 115).

Census of Production data for 1968, now becoming available,
suggests that the effect of regional policy since 1963, with investment
incentives which favour Clydeside over the rest of Scotland for two
years and over the non-development areas for the entire period,
plus the more rigorous application of Industrial Development
Certificate policy after 1964 has led to relatively greater investment
than that in the UK as a whole, but that this has not substantially
strengthened the competitive position of manufacturing industry on
Clydeside, which on average remains relatively weak. Policies to
deal with such a situation must be preceded by diagnosis and it
would be naïve to expect one single explanation to suffice. For long
one explanation was widely accepted; West Central Scotland had
too much 'heavy industry' and too many 'old industries' (steel.
shipbuilding and coal were the usual examples) and was suffering
from the run-down (often accepted as inevitable) of these industries.
A most important outcome of recent studies has been to demonstrate that such a structural explanation can account for less than
half of the total decline of jobs. To illustrate, 'between 1959 and
1968 total employment declined by more than 10,000, a worse trend
than that experienced in any other assisted region of the UK' and yet

if industries in the West Central Scotland had done as well as
their national counterparts ... an extra 43,000 jobs would have
been gained. This 'local deficiency' in employment
performance contrasts markedly with the rest of Scotland, Wales,
Northern Ireland and Northern England, all of which gained
employment more rapidly than their industrial structures
would have suggested.[10]

With structure only part of the explanation attention is turned to
other possible weaknesses, but most of these do not appear to
explain much of the relatively poor performance. Transport costs
have not been given the attention they deserve, and there are
reasons for believing that these have at least added to the difficulties
of some industries and firms. Otherwise it seems reasonable to
endorse the view that neither the region's investment record, the
supply of business finance to firms in the region or of any peculiarity
in the size of these firms are major causes of the economic difficulties of West Central Scotland. Given this, the researchers have

been left with behaviouralist possibilities, difficult to test and extremely sensitive to advance publicly because they appear to criticise those who live and work in the area. To say that industrial relations, management and entrepreneurship could be improved is unexceptionable, but to say that they have contributed to the region's poor economic performance is seen as laying the blame on powerful groups and personalities. The industrial relations issue is more easily subject to demonstration. Statistics for days lost in strikes are only one measure of poor industrial relations, but an important one, and these indicate that between 1960 and 1968 and after adjusting for differences in industrial structure the days lost per annum per 1,000 employees in West Central Scotland were about 75 per cent above the UK average for these years. This picture is not a uniform one, however, with only 14 of the 23 industries covered having a worse strike record in West Central Scotland than in the UK as a whole, and the differences between sub-regions ranging all the way from 10 days per annum per 1,000 employees in one sub-region to 320 days in another (both figures again adjusted to remove the influence of differences in industrial structure). Whatever else one concludes from such divergences in the figures it seems clear that to look for a single explanation in the Scottish character, the alleged disputatiousness of the Celt, the leadership of the Scottish unions or even the long arm of industrial history and a culture-lag from the 1930s, would be misplaced. More detailed examination of industries and firms, and of specific disputes, is required and my own preference would be for what is called 'action research', research sponsored, guided and in part conducted by those who are capable of applying its results if they so wish. The parties to industrial relations must sit down together to discuss why things go wrong, decide on if and how their hypothesis could be tested and ultimately on what policy and actions follow from the outcome of their deliberations. Such an approach is full of difficulties and pitfalls but as a short run antidote to the area's reputation and as a possible way of removing, in the longer run, the objective causes of the more wasteful features of industrial conflict, this 'action research' approach seems to offer more prospects of success than any other.

Turning now to the view that management weaknesses have contributed to the poor economic performance of West Central Scotland, we are faced with even more formidable problems both of establishing whether this is so and of formulating policies for improvement. The exploration begins from the weakness or incompleteness of alternative explanations and then sifts somewhat varied pieces of evidence, none of which is or could be conclusive, but

which when taken together add some weight to the initial hypothesis
A rather similar difficulty has been encountered by economic his
torians who have sought to explain particular developments by the
personality factors of a nation.[11] Neither the difficulty of establishing
such a hypothesis nor the fact that it can be abused constitutes a
legitimate reason for discarding it. Every piece of evidence which
does seem relevant supports the view that the general quality of
management is, on average, below that of the UK. The long-term
impact of self-selective emigration coupled with the smaller propor
tion of high level managerial functions would be likely to produce
this result, and the difficulties of recruitment together with th
tendencies for managerial salaries in industry to be somewhat lowe
also suggests that this is so. With such inconclusive evidence it i
probably best to maintain agnosticism on the question of how fa
managerial deficiencies have contributed to West Central Scotland'
problems, but at the same time to assert that any improvements i
managerial skills which policy can induce or assist must contribute
to an improvement in the area's economic performance. How the
are such improvements to be brought about?

Firstly, and on the supply side, a change in attitude toward
management. Scotland probably suffers from a more acute form o
the more general reservations which young people have abou
careers in management. Scottish education has been more parenta
than societal, with parental values and ambitions leaning toward
teaching, the church, the civil service and the professions and awa
from business. This has reinforced the reservations of the young an
appears to have dampened the enthusiasm of the most highl
qualified for management training and employment.

Secondly, on the demand side—and apart from what reforn
industry might have to make to overcome reservations of the kin
just referred to—limited opportunities for entry to managerial job
and the acute scarcity of career structures which go right to the to
without requiring the people concerned to move permanently awa
from Scotland have affected the situation in the past and continu
to do so, with diminishing force in the lower echelons of recruit
ment and with increasing force in the upper reaches of management
To improve the situation some reorganisation of the administration o
industry involving devolution and redeployment of central decision
taking is necessary. Such reorganisation could be brought about i
a number of ways including a modest merger movement which swim
against the stream to the extent of having more Scottish based com
panies take over companies and plants in other parts of the UK. Allie
to this a speeding up of the process of managerial improvement i
indigenous industry is necessary, similar to that which can follo

upon a merger or on advice from outside. Such approaches require the initiative of an agency along merchant bank lines, similar to the Industrial Reorganisation Corporation but with terms of reference which include the strengthening of Scottish based industry. There are other important elements in the necessary policy package, including more attention to manpower planning and training aimed at smoothing adjustment and stimulating efficiency, and a rapid extension of post-experience management education. This is the appropriate point at which to relate the old-established problems of West Central Scotland to the new developments in oil.

The discovery of oil has opened out exciting new opportunities and prospects for the Scottish economy. It is important, however, not to get these opportunities out of perspective, at least as far as job opportunities are concerned. There has been a decline of over 100,000 in emloyment in Scotland over the last decade and in West Central Scotland alone there are many jobs now held which will disappear over the next decade, perhaps as many as 130,000. The number of jobs direct and indirect, arising in Scotland from oil by the early 1980s is unlikely to exceed 60,000, around a quarter of these will have a life expectancy of under ten years, and the majority will terminate well before the end of this century. As far as employment is concerned, therefore, oil brings partial relief and a breathing space in which to find more lasting solutions. Yet this is not the impression the general public have, and there are dangers that expectations have been raised to such a pitch that the will to tackle the fundamental problems of industrial restructuring and raising efficiency will be weakened. Let us—and this applies with special force to the UK Government—avoid the singular folly of those Eskimos who in this century 'became so convinced of the imminence of the millennium that they stopped hunting and ate into their stores of food'.[12] Without a drop of oil yet ashore and no certainty about how much of the potentially massive revenue might be spent in and on Scotland, Scots are indulging in a kind of cargo-cult believing that somewhere out there there are people and resources which will shortly arrive amongst us and solve our problems. There are dangers for the national psychology in this.

With the problems of change which oil developments bring—industrial, environmental and psychological—added to the problems which existed before, it seems clear that one inevitable element in the Scottish future is more 'policy' and therefore more government, and it is this which increases the need for changes in the administration of Scotland.

Complete independence is attractive because it appears to be clear-cut. The distinction is more apparent than real, however, as

the number and range of issues which independent governments
operating in these islands would have to consult together on is such
that independence could involve almost as much harmonisation as
would devolution. A much stronger case for independence is that it
could provide a better bargaining base from which to carry out
such harmonisation, particularly when backed by the rights to oil
and oil revenues which national sovereignty would bring. But with
the continuous need for harmonisation, plus the short life (in
historical terms) of oil developments perhaps it is the renegotiation
of the Treaty of Union rather than its break-up which should be the
aim, and in practice that is what Kilbrandon and devolution involve.
The importance of harmonising policies within a United Kingdom
in which legislative authority is more widely developed than it is at
present cannot be overstressed. Without it a rational approach to the
regulation of our economic affairs would be impossible. The spill-
over effects of English and Welsh decisions on Scotland and of
Scottish decisions on England and Wales would be too great, and
the inefficiencies which could arise from entirely separate decision-
taking uniformed by the current intention of the other governments,
together require some permanent system of communication, consultation and joint decision-taking, some central authority in other
—less fashionable—words. It is a mistake to build on the experience
of Bannockburn, Hampden Park and Murrayfield and believe that
in economic relations Scotland and England are playing a zero-sum
game.

Devolution can meet the need for harmonisation but it can be
argued that the greater scope for pressure group activity in a more
open system with legislative powers devolved to a Scottish Parliament would make rational decision-taking more difficult. Democracy puts a higher value on the diffusion of power and the curbing
of arbitrary authority than on economic rationality, but an effective
democracy may approximate a more broadly defined rationality—a
social cost-benefit rationality—than would the most dedicated and
rationally calculating group of executives one might wish for as
occupants of St. Andrew's House. In a situation of conflicting
interest groups the search for a complete and perfect rationality
measured in terms of economic efficiency is fruitless. When the
concept of rationality is extended to include social as well as economic costs and benefits a perfect solution is even more unlikely.
But can we realistically expect decision-taking at the level of a
community or a society to pass rigorous tests which fail a tennis
club committee deciding on how to meet the competing demands of
social tennis, team tennis and practice and the coaching of juveniles?
With the certainty of more rather than less government intervention

in Scotland in future it is the need to diffuse power and to have
more open and effective probing of the necessarily imperfect process of striking a balance between conflicting interests much more
than short-term considerations of how to derive a larger benefit
from the wind-fall gain of oil revenues which makes the case for
the devolution of both legislative and executive power within a
British harmonising framework. With public expenditure in Scotland
now in excess of £2,500m. per annum, decisions about how to
allocate this between alternative uses should be taken closer to the
purposes on which the money is to be spent and in full view of
the people whose interests the expenditure is intended to serve. And
having to argue these matters out amongst ourselves could help
free us from the severe limitation on our ability for creative
thinking which arise whenever an indentifiable group depends for
its welfare upon the decisions of a larger group of which it is
part.

We have been looking at the pressures for change on the structure
of industry and government of a small geographical area, pressures
which arise from a rather limited but important concurrence of
problems. A wider horizon is needed, however, for all industrial
societies are faced with the need for adaptation and change. Who
today can be certain about the shape of the future, even twenty
years ahead? Who believes that the next fifty years will be 'much
the same' as the last fifty? And although the need for change may
be accepted, what confidence can we have that the changes which
transpire will be designed to serve this need? Change can 'happen
casually'. Different commentators have called this the 'accidental
century', the 'age of discontinuity', and the 'unprepared society'.
We again go back two centuries to the Scottish moralists and their
notion of 'unintended social outcomes'. One justified concern to
which increased voice has recently been given is that inflation will
encourage the adoption of policy measures which will have consequences much more far reaching than are intended or even recognised: for example that wage and price controls, seen as short-term
policies, could carry us—step by step—too far down the road to the
corporate state to make the return easy or even possible.

The balance achieved between a rapidly developing industrial
society and a pluralist political system is a delicate one and could be
easily upset. Industrial society, and in particular the division of
labour, the emphasis upon growth, and the emerging mass culture,
have all sharply challenged traditional attitudes to the individual
family, state and church—and these traditional attitudes have given
way or adapted faced by these pressures. Very recently social
scientists—including a few economists—have challenged the wide

I

acceptance given to economic growth as the proper—even inevitable —aim of societies. In this they are fully justified. The criticisms of those other economists who have argued that it is not our place to be for or against the selection of aims overlook the extent to which implicitly at least growth has been a built-in aim of most economic policies, unchallenged by the conventional wisdom until very recently. It also overlooks that since Keynes's *General Theory* in 1936 most economists have abandoned the allegedly neutral aim of equilibrium for macro-economic policy, and accepted the unavoidably value-loaded aim of 'full employment'. The artificially created oil crisis of autumn 1973 greatly increased the appeal of the Club of Rome view of things that economic growth must come to an end, taken more as a matter of fact than of values. Somewhat paradoxically the onset of acute scarcity is to herald not only the end of the world as we have known it, but more particularly the end of the economists' view of the world. Other economists have made counter argument to this view, and my own allegiance is to those technological optimists who believe that 'something (indeed a very large number of things) will turn up'. Such optimism must not be mistaken for judgement, and the only credential I can offer is that it is not my universal state of mind. I was a pessimist when only ten years ago we were being told that with the help of automation and numerical control systems scarcity was about to be abolished and the age of plenty was at hand. On the pessimistic side, however, it is interesting to note that whereas improvements in the efficiency with which natural resources are used has been increasing over a wide range this has not been so for oil or for natural gas, with GNP per cubic foot of natural gas used *falling* by $2\frac{1}{2}$ per cent per annum in the USA between 1951 and 1970.[13] Thus in the fuel sector, unless increases in efficiency come quickly and the stock of existing fuels is substantially increased by discovery we do depend upon a technological break-through if a fuel bottleneck is not to throttle off further growth at some point in the first half of the next century. It is difficult to avoid one's prejudices and preferences affecting the view adopted in this 'growth, slow growth, zero growth' controversy. I react against the emphasis on 'the human condition' and 'the predicament of mankind' as 'spaceship earth' gyrates into the twenty-first century and the associated tendency to lose sight of the problem of particular individuals, groups and peoples who deserve help in the here and now. And when it comes to taking the longer view I prefer an approach which allows more scope for human influence and development than does the mechanical extrapolation of the systems analysts. The anti-growth lobbyists have been cast in the role of guardians of human values against the relentless intention of modern societies to produce and consume more, an intention enthusiastically endorsed by economists, yet the 'doomsday models' depend upon an assumed inflexibility of behaviour more appropriate to robots than to humans. Economists have come off badly in this debate because, in their rejection of doomsday models, they have restricted their critique to the probability of new discoveries, the certainty of price changes affecting rates of consumption of raw materials, the possibility of policies to curtail or eliminate pollution and the like. All of these are valid, but not enough. Underlying the appeal of the anti-growth argument is the distaste for modern industrial society which, in its different forms, unites sections of society widely separated in education, occupation and social status. Modern industrial society is tolerated only because it delivers the goods. Keynes put it this way: 'For at least another hundred years we must pretend to ourselves and to everyone that fair is foul and foul is fair; for foul is useful and fair is not.'[14] There are two errors in this approach. First it does not make clear that society is not faced with a stark choice between the quantity of goods and services on the one hand and the quality of life on the other, but may strike a balance and within that balance reduce the 'foulness' of the means by which the ends of production and a better life are attained. Secondly, and more seriously, it suggests that after more than a century of social life conditioned by acceptance of what is foul as fair, a transformation could take place, the old values and attitudes being rapidly shed and replaced by something akin to their opposites. Here Keynes was exemplifying the insensitivity of much of the thinking of economists on the problems of growth, to the existence of powerful psychological and sociological brakes upon the necessary changes in attitudes and values. The shift to a political economics, which Keynes set in motion nearly forty years ago has to go much further if economists are to help people affect the future of industrial society in ways other than as unintended by-products of a commitment to maximising growth or employment. The argument is not that economists should determine the macro-goals, but that they should accept and even encourage the explicit adoption *by society and through the political process* of a hierarchy of goals which becomes a datum for their work as economists. This hierarchy of goals will include social elements as well as economic ones, and economists and other social scientists should be able to suggest the extent to which these interrelate and in particular how individual goals affect other goals with a higher place in the hierarchy. The problems of how collective choice can be exercised and of how far the micro-goals of individuals and units whose consent and participation is a necessary condition for the attainment of the macro-goals are compatible with the hierarchy of macro-goals must be tackled by political scientists, economists, sociologists and others. Politics and the political system play the central role in the formulation of macro-goals, with the social scientist helping society in a 'staff' capacity to reformulate the hierarchy of goals (and the associated time scales). Unless the political system sets goals the economist will fall back on his expertise in a narrowly defined area of output and growth. We have at present a widespread recognition of the inevitability of social change and an absence of political discussion about the alternative societies which could emerge. There will alweys be unintended social outcomes but one purpose of social science is to increase the influence of the purposive over the instinctive and to evolve motivations which align the instinctive behaviour of individuals and micro-units with the macro-goals they have helped to formulate. A political system which sets goals and an economic system which is willing to serve them must come together if an effective political economy is to develop.

The burden of my criticism of economists—and it is, of course, self-criticism also—is that we are dangerously and narrowly over-specialised and fail to 'connect' with some of the new trends in industrial society which it is our responsibility to contribute to. Where does this criticism relate to the Scottish situation?

Firstly, the magnitude of our economic problems, in West Central in particular, makes it clear that we need change—and not just structural change but behavioural change. Secondly, we are about to benefit from an unexpected windfall gain of (historically) short duration, but both large enough in financial terms and long-lasting enough in time to allow us to make changes in rather favourable circumstances. Thirdly, Scots have some capacity for experimentation and initiative and the combination of need and opportunity might create circumstances in which we could apply this capacity to experimenting with changes in the character of industrial society. Lastly, our tradition in the social sciences—and in social philosophy and political economy in particular—has perhaps left enough behind it to encourage our social scientists to contribute to such a process of experimentation and change. To do so economists would have to accept David Hume's insistence that 'Reason is, and ought only to be the slave of the passions and can never pretend to any other office than to serve and obey them.'[15] A broader perspective of the behavioural element in economic choice is needed. In *The Place of Science in Modern Civilisation* published in 1919, Thorstien Veblen wrote:

Any science such as economics, which has to do with human conduct becomes a genetic enquiry into the human scheme of life; and where, as in economics, the subject of enquiry is the conduct of man in his dealing with the material means of life the science is necessarily an enquiry into the life history of material civilisation . . .[16]

At the heart of the life history of material civilisation is human behaviour and economists must acknowledge the many ways in which institutional arrangements and ideological preconceptions and passions can affect and change such behaviour. Human nature was Hume's central interest and the wealth of nations was Smith's. It is time to bring them more closely together again if we are to have guidance from a political economy of change.

Notes

1. A. Smith, *Inquiry into the Nature & Causes of the Wealth of Nations,* IV (p. 55 in Vol. III of 1819 edition).
2. L. Robbins, *The Nature & Significance of Economic Science* 1932, p. 69.
3. L. Robbins, *Politics & Economics*, Macmillan, 1973, p. 23.
4. A. Ferguson, *An Essay on the History of Civil Society, 1767,* Univ. Press, Edinburgh, 1966, p. 122.
5. L. Robbins, *Politics & Economics*, Macmillan, 1973, p. 23.
6. H. Clegg, *How to Run an Incomes Policy*, Heinemann, 1971.
7. *Report of a Court of Inquiry into a Dispute between the National Coal Board and the National Union of Mineworkers* under the Chairmanship of the Rt. Hon. Lord Wilberforce, HMSO, 1972, Cmd. 4903.
8. J. M. Keynes, *The Economic Consequences of Mr. Churchill*, Macmillan, 1925.
9. D. Lockwood, in *Sociological Review, Monograph No. 8,* 1964.
10. *West Central Scotland—A Programme of Action,* 1974, p. 8, and see also: Cameron G., 'Economic Analysis of a Declining Urban Area', *Scottish Journal of Political Economy*, Nov. 1971; Randall J., 'Shift Share Analysis', SJPE., February 1973.
11. See, in particular, Hagen E. E., On the Theory of Social Change, London, 1964; and 'British Personality and the Industrial Revolution' in Burns T., and Saul S. B., *Social Theory of Economic Change*, University of Edinburgh, 1965.
12. P. Worsley, *The Trumpet Shall Sound*, 1st edn., Macgibbon & Kee, 1957, p. 225.
13. R. Solow, in *The Economic Growth Controversy*, ed. Weintraub A. and Others, Macmillan, 1974.
14. J. M. Keynes, 'Economic Possibilities for our Grandchildren' (1930) in *Essays in Persuasion*, Macmillan, 1931, p. 372.
15. D. Hume, *A Treatise of Human Nature*, Vol. II, Longmans, 1898, p. 195.
16. T. Veblen, *The Place of Science in Modern Civilization*, p. 241.

10

North Sea Oil and the Scottish Economy

D. I. Mackay*

What I shall attempt is very much a personal view of some of the questions which seem to me important. My objective is a modest one, to promote discussion, rather than to provide many firm answers.

The questions asked depend on the standpoint of the observer and my choice of title indicates that I am particularly concerned with the impact of oil development in Scotland. For this I make no apologies: to understand the strong emotions, the hopes, aspirations and fears which this subject raises above all others in contemporary Scotland, we have to recognise that to Scots, North Sea oil has a very special significance. It is not simply a matter of offsetting the terrifying burden which the recent rises in crude oil prices have imposed on the current amount of the balance of payments. It is much more than this: a possible escape from the depressing economic record of Scotland over the last half century. It is seen as a means of redressing the balance of economic, industrial and commercial power within the UK in favour of Scotland. This being so, North Sea oil is more a question of political economy than of economic science.

Such a viewpoint is understandable. Throughout the postwar period Scotland has been a slow growing region in a slow growing

* Professor of Political Economy, University of Aberdeen; Lister Lecture 1974. This paper has been heavily influenced by discussions with my colleagues in the North Sea Study Group, the Department of Political Economy, Aberdeen University—Professor M. Gaskin, G. A. Mackay, N. Trimble and A. Moir. But I must add the usual disclaimer that none of my colleagues are responsible for the particular views expressed, nor do these reflect in any sense the opinions of the Scottish Office which has financed the work of the group. The draft of this paper was completed on 29 July 1974 and I have left it unchanged except for some minor amendments which reflect recent developments.

national economy. The early 1960s were the trough and subsequently there has been a clearly discernable improvement in Scotland's relative economic performance as Figure 1 shows (see p. 128). The gap between Scottish and British employment and per capita income has narrowed and the unemployment relative has improved markedly with the result that emigration has decreased. But, while change may have been in the desired direction, the pace of change throughout the 1960s was disappointingly slow. Very simply, Scotland had still not solved the problem of finding a replacement for the old trinity of shipbuilding and engineering, iron and steel and coal, which fired her economic growth in the late nineteenth and early twentieth centuries.

The question then is whether North Sea oil and gas and their associated developments offer a new watershed, a new dynamic which will bring a major improvement in economic performance and remove the long-standing disadvantages in terms of low income, high unemployment and heavy emigration. My view is that this may happen, but only if we correctly perceive the nature of the economic benefits which will arise from North Sea oil and have the political will to use these in particular directions.

One final word of warning. The chief characteristic of what follows is the considerable uncertainty and doubt attaching to most of the statements I will make. Given the nature of North Sea oil activities only the historian will be able to form a clear picture of its economic effects. Policy has to be made in the present on a very insecure basis. For the analyst this is frustrating and he may find little to please him in the following discussion. Hopefully, a wider audience will find something of interest.

Some Economic Effects

The current inputs required to obtain North Sea oil are much smaller than the final value of the product. This can be illustrated by reference to the three fields for which fairly detailed estimates of likely capital expenditure are available—Auk, Piper and Forties. I estimate that development expenditure might amount to some $90m for Auk, $500m for Piper and $1,500m for Forties. At peak production these fields are likely to yield 40,000, 225,000 and 400,000 barrels a day. The current price of Arabian Light (cif, UK) is in the region of $10–$11 a barrel. Given the excellent quality of North Sea crude and its proximity to the main consuming market this would seem to suggest that we should value North Sea crude at some $11 a barrel as long as present oil prices are maintained. On

Figure 1

Comparative Economic Performance of Scotland

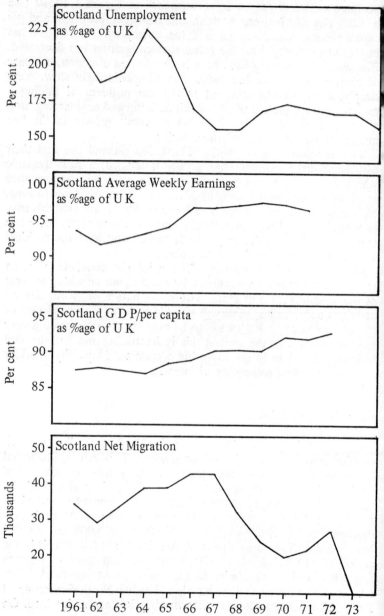

this assumption, at peak production,[1] the gross annual value of output will be $160m for Auk, $740m for Piper and $1,600m for Forties.

In making this type of analysis we have to bear in mind that capital expenditure is incurred some time in advance of any revenue flow and that the risks involved in North Sea oil operations are considerably greater than those in normal commercial and industrial activities. Nonetheless, the chief economic characteristic of North Sea oil is that value added accounts for a very high proportion of final sales value. The owner of the natural resource can then command a high economic rent and this is why the formulation of an appropriate taxation system, by which we mean virtually any system other than the one first adopted, is of prime importance. It also follows from this that the chief significance of indigenous supplies is not the direct impact on employment and output, but the fact that self-sufficiency, which seems likely to be achieved over 1978–80, will offset the burden placed on the balance of payments current account by the recent rise in crude oil prices. In estimating North Sea oil reserves and the likely flow rate of production, considerable differences of opinion are inevitable. Our own estimates of known reserves and of possible production (on the rather heroic assumption that no further slippage will occur) are shown in Tables 1 and 2 (see pp. 130 and 131). The reader familiar with official estimates will see that these forecasts, which were made earlier this year, are significantly higher than those put forward by the Government in its recent 'Brown Book'.[2]

Taking 158m tons as the 1980 output of oil, and assuming that 1974 oil prices are maintained, then the annual value of such a level of production would be in the region of £5,800m. Allowing for the increased cost of oil imports (for simplicity I assume that North Sea oil will be exported and that we will continue to import crude from the Middle East, an assumption which will probably be near enough to the truth) then the surplus on the visible balance of trade in crude oil will be more than £2,000m annually. Making some further guesses about the input content of equipment and services necessary to obtain North Sea oil, direct investment from abroad in North Sea activities and interest and profit remitted overseas, we might arrive at a surplus in the current and capital account of the 'oil' balance of payments of some £1,300m by 1980. Without North Sea oil the deficit on the 'oil' balance of payments might have been some £4,000m. UK tax on North Sea oil operations is likely, given the nature of the proposals recently put forward,[3] to be more than £3,000m a year by 1980.

While all these figures are only rough guesses at the likely outcome they do give an indication of the economic importance of North Sea discoveries. The improvement in the balance of payments will allow any given balance of payments target to be achieved at a higher level of employment. It should also assist the UK to finance the oil deficit until self-sufficiency is reached and to achieve the trade surplus which will be necesary in the 1980s to

Table 1

Estimated recoverable reserves of known commercial oil fields

FIELD	BLOCK(S)	LICENSEE	ESTIMATED RESERVES (*million barrels*)
Alwyn	3/14	Total/Elf group	300
Argyll	30/24	Hamilton group	150
Auk	30/16	Shell/Esso	100
Beryl	9/13	Mobil group	500
Brent	211/29	Shell/Esso	2,000
	3/4	Texaco	
Claymore	14/9	Occidental group	600
Cormorant	211/26	Shell/Esso	400
Dunlin	211/23	Shell/Esso	600
	211/24	Conoco/Gulf/NCB	
Forties	21/10	BP	1,850
	22/6	Shell/Esso	
Hutton	211/28	Conoco/Gulf/NCB	500
	211/27	Amoco group	
Maureen	16/29	Phillips group	450
Montrose	22/18	GC/Amoco	200
	22/17	GC/Amoco	
Ninian	3/8	BP Ranger group	2,100
	3/3	Burmah group	
Piper	15/7	Occidental group	800
Thistle	211/18	Burmah group	750
Heather	2/5	Unocal group	350
Andrew	16/28	BP	400
Magnus	211/12	BP	750
Others*			1,000
Total			13,800

* Discoveries in blocks 20/5 (Texaco), 21/1 (Transworld), 9/8 (Hamilton) and 9/13 (Mobil) for which no information is yet available.

Table 2

Estimated production rates from known oil fields
(*thousands of barrels per day*)

FIELD	1975	1976	1977	1978	1979	1980	1981	1982	1983
Alwyn			25	80	100	100	100	90	80
Argyll	30	60	60	60	60	50	50	50	—
Auk	20	40	40	40	35	35	35	35	—
Beryl		60	120	150	150	150	135	120	110
Brent		75	125	250	370	480	480	480	480
Claymore			25	60	150	150	150	150	135
Cormorant				40	75	75	75	68	60
Dunlin			30	100	125	125	125	125	110
Forties	50	200	400	400	400	360	324	292	262
Hutton			25	60	120	120	120	110	100
Maureen			25	60	100	100	100	100	90
Montrose		30	50	50	50	50	45	40	35
Ninian				50	200	350	500	500	500
Piper	20	100	225	225	225	225	202	182	164
Thistle			50	100	200	200	200	180	160
Heather				25	100	100	100	100	90
Andrew				25	100	100	100	100	90
Magnus				50	150	200	200	200	180
Others					50	200	400	400	400
Totals	120	565	1,200	1,825	2,760	3,170	3,441	3,322	3,046

service and reduce the debt incurred in supporting that deficit. Hence, indirectly, there may be some favourable impact on the aggregate level of employment in the long run, but this is likely to be relatively small and to be spread across all regions.

There is, however, another effect which flows from the direct impacts of the capital expenditures necessary to obtain North Sea oil and gas. While these are necessarily less important than the effects discussed above, it is of particular interest to us here today as it is these direct effects which may bring particular benefits to Scotland. Moreover, because the direct impacts are felt in an area of relatively high unemployment and low labour activity rates it will be possible to increase the aggregate level of employment and output in the United Kingdom. If North Sea oil discoveries had been made off a region with full employment then the increased employment in oil related activities would have been at the expense of employment and output in other sectors of the economy. To maintain the same overall pressure of demand would have required corrective action through fiscal and monetary policy. In Scotland with a level of unemployment significantly above the national average it should be possible to bring into employment people who would otherwise be out of work. Thus, the opportunity cost of additional employment in Scotland is much lower than it would be in a fully employed region and admits a net increase in national employment and output.

The extent to which this can happen will depend on the level of expenditure necessary to obtain oil and gas, on the competitive capacity of Scottish industry and on the absorbtive capacity of the economy. But to say this merely begins another list of questions rather than providing any answers. What will be the rate and the duration of expenditure and associated employment in exploration, drilling and production? Can our industry adapt quickly to the needs of North Sea oil and gas, or will much of the demand for equipment and services be met by suppliers outside the UK? Will the impacts be unevenly distributed within Scotland so that the major benefits are felt by areas which already have low level unemployment and only a small labour force catchment area to draw upon? If so, what implications does this have for physical, economic and regional policy? In the remainder of this paper I shall look at these questions, but it may be useful to precede that discussion by a quick review of the current situation.

The Present Position

I shall start from a simple taxonomy of North Sea oil activities.[4] At the risk of doing considerable violence to the complexity of the oil industry in practice, four types of activity are distinguished:

(1) Operational activities and related services—exploration, drilling, production and back-up services, e.g. catering, maintenance and jobbing work, supply vessels etc.

(2) Production of equipment and materials—oil rigs, oil tools, drilling materials, production platforms, module construction and supply boats.

(3) The processing of oil and gas and associated industrial developments.

(4) The construction of permanent production facilities (e.g. oil terminals, gas terminals, refineries, pipelines and the construction activities involved in providing the associated infrastructure—housing, schools, roads, harbours, airports etc.).

It is clear that operational activities and related services have concentrated in the ports along the east coast of Scotland—in Aberdeen particularly, but also in Dundee, Montrose, Peterhead, Wick and the Orkney and Shetland Islands. These will continue to remain the chief centres in the future. There may be some relative shift of servicing activity in favour of bases in the North and the Shetlands, but the major centre will remain Aberdeen which has become the main supply base and the administrative centre for North Sea oil activities.

The second category of activities is even more diffuse and locational requirements vary considerably from one item to the next. The most important item is productuion platforms. The IMEG Report estimated that expenditure from North Sea oil activities might amount to £270–£300m per annum by 1980 and that of this no less than £80–£85m would be on platforms.[5] There are obvious advantages in siting platform production yards fairly close to the oil fields, but different types of platform have very different locational requirements. In particular, certain concrete designs require very deep and sheltered water close in shore and such sites are found in Britain only on the north-west coast of Scotland. Piled platforms, which are steel fabricated, can be built on a much wider range of locations and have all been located on the east coast. Evidently the spatial distribution of employment from this activity will depend on the number and timing of the platforms ordered, the distribution of demand between steel, concrete and the new hybrid designs and the extent of competition from foreign yards. Given the importance of this type of activity and the substantial impacts which it can have on the communities affected I have thought it worthwhile to set out in Table 3 (see p. 134) some estimates of the likely demand for platforms which is the first step to calculating the eventual impacts. The reader is warned that the estimates are derived from a process which frequently requires assumptions or guesses made on the basis of rather slender information. He should therefore consult the particular paper from which the estimates are drawn before coming to any final conclusion. One last point might be made in this connection. Given this forward view of demand then it appears likely that platform production might peak sometime in 1976–7 and decline thereafter.

The remainder of our second category of activities differ from production platform construction in that they are not location specific. The mobility of much of this equipment means that it can move from one offshore area to another and the ease of movement implies greater competition from overseas manufacturers. For example, almost all the rigs currently operating in the North Sea were built outwith the UK and it appears probable that more than 90 per cent of the value of orders placed for rigs, supply boats and lay barges, have been with foreign manufacturers. All in all, it would appear that we are still a good way short of IMEG's optimistic

Table 3

Estimated Demand for Production Platforms from Existing Fields

FIELD	WATER DEPTH (feet)	PEAK FLOW RATES (barrels per day)	NO. OF PLATFORMS ORDERED		PLATFORM ORDERS TO COME		TOTAL	DATE field will be fully operational
			steel	concrete	steel	concrete		
Alwyn	400	100,000				1	1	1979
Argyll	250	50,000			1		1	1974
Auk	275	40,000	1				1	1974
Beryl	385	100–150,000	1	1			2	1977
Brent	460	400–600,000	1	3		1	5	1977
Claymore	375	100–150,000				1	1	1980
Cormorant	500	50,000		1			1	1978
Dunlin	500	150–250,00		1		1	2	1978
Forties	400	400,000	4				4	1978
Hutton	490	150–250,000				2	2	1978–9
Maureen	325	100–150,000			1		1	1979
Montrose	300	50,000	1				1	1977
Ninian	450	400–600,000				4–5	4–5	1980
Piper	475	225,000	1				1	1977
Thistle	530	100–200,000			1		1	1979
2/5	400–450	75–125,000				1	1	1979
16/28	325	50–100,000			1		1	1980
Totals		2,540,000–3,490,000	8	6	4	12–13	30–31	

Source: G. A. Mackay and N. Trimble, 'The Demand for Production Platforms and Platform Sites', North Sea Study Group

hope that the share of British manufacturers and contractors in the UK North Sea market would rise to some 70 per cent in the late 1970s.

One major reason for this high penetration by overseas suppliers is that the extent and the pace of North Sea oil developments have placed those with acquired skill and know-how in a favourable competitive position. As time passes it must be hoped that manufacturing industry in Britain can adapt to these new needs and the corollary of the competition we experience from foreign manufacturers in the UK sector of the North Sea is that there are other offshore areas in which we might apply the experience obtained in North Sea operations. In Scottish terms, Clydeside would appear to be able to benefit most from this type of development and there are some hopeful indications that traditional engineering and ship-building firms are beginning to break into wider markets. However, some types of production may tend to concentrate on the east coast. This certainly appears to be true of oil tool manufacturing and there does seem to have been a general tendency to underestimate the pull which the external economies of proximity to the oil fields will exert on overseas manufacturers seeking base in this country.

Like much of the equipment and material production, the processing of oil and gas is not tied to oil fields. Indeed, there is a marked tendency to locate downstream activities close to final markets. Many commentators attach substantial hopes to an expansion of refining capacity in Scotland and to the establishment of petrochemical industries using the new resources as feed stocks. Here there are possibilities of oil refining and associated activities in the west of Scotland, Grangemouth, Nigg Bay, even, or so some reports suggest, in the Shetlands and Loch Eriboll. Natural gas discoveries may also have an industrial spin-off and there is a strong possibility of industrial developments associated with the St. Fergus gas terminal. Gas may also prove to be a feed stock for other industries such as steel.

My own view would be that while some of these developments are quite likely the employment they would create would be substantially less than that associated with operational and production activities. A doubling of the capacity of the Grangemouth refinery would cope with the growth of the Scottish market over the remainder of this decade and other oil refinery development would seem to depend largely on servicing the American market with relatively little industrial spin-off. If commercial considerations were paramount then the bulk of North Sea oil seems likely to be refined outside Scotland, and indeed outside the UK, at locations adjacent to major consuming markets on the Continent. However, if the

Government decides that the balance of payments benefit, from the value added in downstream activities, requires refining in the UK, then it has sufficient bargaining power to enforce its decision and this may have an important effect on the locations chosen.

In view of all these uncertainties it is difficult to make any prediction with confidence, but we can obtain some idea of the existing distribution of oil-related employment and of possible increases in employment for those firms which are already established in these activities. These estimates are confined to activities 1–3, what might be called primary employment creation. Subsequently, we shall consider secondary employment created through the multiplier process in the service industries and the employment in construction which comprises both primary and secondary effects. The latest *primary* employment estimates made by the Department of Employment are set out in Table 4 below.

Table 4

Present and Forecast Employment of Companies Engaged in North Sea Oil Activities, June 1974

AREA	PRESENT EMPLOYMENT	FORE-CAST INCREASE	TOTAL
Inverness and Easter Ross	4,860	1,245	6,105
Remainder of Highlands and Islands	470	270	740
North East	4,545	3,690	8,235
Tayside	270	355	625
East Central Scotland	2,275	100	2,375
West Central	2,785[1]	235	3,020
Totals	15,205	5,895	21,110

[1] Including Marathon.

Source: Department of Employment.

These figures are the best measure we have of the employment created by existing oil-related activities, but for a number of reasons, which are inseparable from this type of exercise, they probably underestimate the true position. First, there is always a time lag before employment created by new firms is identified. Second, it is impossible to keep track of the large number of small firms (who are particularly important in operational and servicing activities) and of those firms whose main activity lies elsewhere and who are essentially engaged in sub-contract work for specialist producers. If this is correct then employment in the North East and in the West Central areas will be subject to most downward bias. Indeed, it is extremely difficult to accept the West Central figure at face value as it suggests that discounting Marathon, which is not building rigs for the North Sea, there are less than 1,000 persons engaged in this region in North Sea oil activities.

The forecast increase in Table 4 does not, of course, take account of employment which will arise from new entrants to North Sea oil activities. Developments which already have planning permission may create a further 1,500 jobs, but this does not take full account of employment and production platform construction, oil refining and natural gas treatment, and only a futurologist could predict the developments which will certainly take place in a wide range of offshore engineering. However, taking our courage in both hands it would seem that direct employment in activities 1–3 might amount to 25,000–30,000 at its peak, which will probably be sometime in the late 1970s.[6]

There are still other factors which should also be weighed in the balance. North Sea oil activities will lead directly to a high level of employment in the construction of production facilities—tanker terminals, gas terminals, pipe laying, refineries and other plant. Again, there will be, through a normal Keynesian multiplier process, a series of secondary effects on the service sector and a further wave of construction activities providing the necessary infrastructure. Employment in services and in the construction industry is likely to be on a 1:1 ratio with primary employment,[7] so that total employment creation might be in the range 50,000–60,000.

Up to this point my process of guesstimating has been very mechanical, based on employment which has been created or can be fairly readily foreseen, and then going through the usual arithmetic of the Keynesian income or employment multiplier. But none of this does justice to the complexity of North Sea oil developments, or to the growth dynamic that they might create. As most British economists would readily admit we know very little of how to create economic growth, for which statement there is no better testimony than the frantic search in postwar Britain for some method of improving on our economic performance. But, while economists find it difficult to create growth, they would also find it difficult to make it go away once it occurs. Economic growth appears to be a matter of vicious or virtuous circles and it is difficult to break out of either circle once it is established.

The same comments apply in the regional context. Regional policy, although it has certainly been of considerable assistance to the development areas, has never been able to provide the major

K

structural shift which is necessary to achieve more rapid economic growth. It is this shift which is essential for a fundamental change in the prospects of development areas such as Scotland. Regional policy should not begin and end with the question of manipulating effective demand. What is also required is a change in the pattern of production and in production functions. North Sea oil and gas and its associated developments may provide the missing stimulus, a new industrial base to sustain expansion. But if so, we are talking about what Hicks in the context of the theory of fluctuations,[8] and Wilson, in the context of regional development,[9] called the 'super-multiplier': something more complex, more dynamic and certainly more unpredictable than the simple and mechanistic Keynesian multiplier. Some process like this is certainly at work in those areas of Scotland which have been particularly affected by North Sea oil impacts. It is evident that in a very short space of time business expectations as to the future have been simply transformed and this is apparently influencing a whole range of activities which have little direct connection with North Sea oil. This sort of development is most obvious in the city of Aberdeen. As economists we can do little to analyse or quantify these effects: but we should be prepared to recognise that they exist as they have significant implications for physical and economic planning and for regional policy.

The Distribution of Activity and Likely Future Trends

As can be seen from Table 4 the present employment created by North Sea oil is highly concentrated. The direct employment thus far created in Aberdeen city[10] and in Inverness and the Moray Firth accounts for more than 9,000 jobs, with a forecast increase of a further 4,500 direct jobs for companies which are already established in these areas. This employment increase has occurred in regions which were already showing substantial expansion in the late 1960s. As the combined population of the two areas is only some 300,000 very considerable bottlenecks have arisen in labour supply and in housing particularly. The pace and scale of change have been considerable and it might be useful to illustrate this briefly using the North East and Aberdeen city as an example.

Employment began to increase in Aberdeen and the North East in 1969, a period over which employment in Britain was falling quite sharply. The initial expansion accelerated sharply from 1971 with the first impact from North Sea oil. From 1971 more than 200 companies have established offices in the city. In 1972 existing office space was 140,000 sq. ft. Since then 17,000 sq. ft. has been completed, a further 29,000 sq. ft. is under construction, sites have been cleared for an additional 17,000 sq. ft. and proposed developments amount to 33,000 sq. ft. The level of unemployment in the North East was 1½ times the British average in 1969–71, fell to the national mean by 1973 and has been below the national level throughout 1974. In Aberdeen city the level of unemployment is now 40 per cent below the Scottish rate and, at the last count, was slightly below the level for south-east England. As far as I can tell this is the first time since detailed unemployment statistics became available in 1924 that the unemployment rate in any area of Scotland has been as low as the rate for south-east England.

The best estimates we can make, and these are probably very conservative, suggest that given no constraints on labour supply and housing, then employment in Aberdeen city will grow from 109,000 in 1971 to 135,000 in 1981, which will require an increase in population of 35,000. The absolute rate of growth is high even compared to that achieved by the New Towns established in Scotland since 1945. In terms of housing requirements we have estimated a housing 'need' of 16,000 houses over 1972–6, an average rate of building which is significantly above the peak rate achieved previously. Over the first two years of this five-year programme the number of houses actually completed was only 3,000 or 38 per cent of the 'required' building rate.

Similar statistics can be produced for the other areas, such as the Moray Firth and the Shetlands, which have borne the major impacts to North Sea oil. However, the stability and the duration of employment differs considerably from one type of activity and area to the next. Generalisation is difficult, but it is reasonably accurate to say that in the north and the west the employment effects have a narrow industrial base and fall on much smaller communities with small labour markets, a limited range of services and poor infrastructure. The result is that there is a real danger that these communities may face sharp fluctuations in employment and that the duration of any employment will be relatively short lived: or at least that it will not provide a base for a wider industrial and economic expansion. The classic example is the planning application for production platform sites at Drumbuie. Many authorities might accept the need for these sites given the swing. In concrete platforms and the balance of payments costs of delays, not to speak of the need to meet Norwegian competition if we are to maximise the direct employment effects of North Sea oil developments. Yet it is extremely difficult to believe, despite some 'expert' testimony at the planning inquiry to the contrary, that Drumbuie could become a substantial growth point. A production platform site, whatever its merits on the grounds of national interest, would be a 'cathedral in the desert'. Its multiplier effects would be extremely limited and it would leave behind not a growth complex, but simply a hole in the ground which is often euphemistically referred to as a marina.

It is clear that North Sea oil and gas developments will in the future have a major effect on the distribution of employment and population. The question then arises as to how we can assist this transition to take place smoothly. What implications does it have for regional policy? How should the costs and benefits be shared between local communities, incoming firms and the central government? What are the problems which prevent labour market adjustment and, associated with this, are there real supply constraints in the construction industry which will prevent or make difficult the changes in employment and population distribution which appear necessary? In answering these questions we must always bear in mind the fact that the nature of the problem does vary considerably from area to area. Employment in the Moray Firth region, because of the dominance of two major production platform builders, is likely to be subject to much more violent cyclical fluctuation than in Aberdeen. Similarly, in the Shetlands, there will be a high peak in activity generated from the construction of permanent production facilities and some seasonal variation in supply boat movements.[11] In Drumbuie, if planning permission is granted, and possibly at some sites in Argyll, we will witness the formation of what are virtually company towns dependent on one type of activity of limited duration. The economic and physical planning problems involved are again quite different at a site such as Hunterston where production platform facilities are also likely to be established, but where there is a large labour market to draw upon and the possibility of alternative employment following from production platform activity. These differences have some significant regional, economic and physical planning implications. We cannot examine all of these here, but there are three questions I would like to highlight—the type of regional policy which might be appropriate in the Scottish context, the question of financing the major capital expenditures which North Sea oil developments make inevitable and the lessons we might learn from the past application of incomes policy to these areas undergoing substantial and rapid economic change.

What Type of Regional Policy?

The Scots live in a highly industrialised society in a sparsely populated country. More than 80 per cent of the population is concentrated in the narrow central belt. Yet the impact of North Sea oil activities is, for the most part, being felt in areas far removed from Clydeside which contains the heart of the Scottish economic problem of heavy unemployment and high emigration. It is clear that Clydeside in terms of labour supply, housing and other infrastructure has the capacity to accommodate, at significantly lower social cost, greater developments than the Highlands and Islands and the North East. Hence there is a continuing emphasis on steering developments away from the 'pressured' areas towards the central belt and especially to Clydeside. It is this reasoning which underlies the recent decisions to establish the Offshore Supplies Office in Glasgow and the Centre of Drilling Technology in Livingstone, as by any other yardstick they appear bizarre locations. Much the same can be said if, as seems likely, the British National Oil Corporation is steered to Glasgow where the centre of government administration will be away from the administrative centre of the operating companies.

A strong case could be made for following a quite different policy —for concentrating the government offices associated with North Sea oil developments in the locations which are the centre for the activities of the private companies. In this way one might better build up a centre of offshore technology with significant external economies. However, the pressures operating in the other direction are real enough and in any event the precise location of government offices is often much less important than is supposed. Whatever decisions are made about the distribution of civil employment, it is likely that the continued weight of development will work in favour of east-coast sites. This proposition is based on the consideration that many North Sea oil activities are location specific and require a site near or on the oil fields. As a consequence of this many other establishments may be drawn to ports on the east coast because of the external economies—access to buyers and supplier, to technical and commercial information, to a pool of skilled labour—with which we are familiar. There is nothing surprising in the fact that new companies continue to be attached to Aberdeen despite its obvious difficulties in meeting all the demands placed on it and despite the existence of ports like Dundee with substantial harbour capacity, wharfage space, warehousing etc. On the contrary, this continued concentration is likely to intensify because of external economies. We have to adapt to these facts and not to our preconceived notions as to what constitutes a desirable distribution of employment and population.

Following a similar line of argument I would suggest that so long as Scotland needs the incentives provided by regional policy, they should be made available to all areas within Scotland. We should resist the argument put forward from a number of quarters, particularly *The Economist*, that some areas should be de-scheduled so that development area assistance is concentrated on those places which experience high unemployment. It would be a retrograde step to go back to a system of classification reminiscent of the development districts where only the areas of high unemployment receive assistance. The objections to this approach are well known. In brief, such areas are very often the least attractive and offer little possibility of rapid economic growth. This is not a suggestion for positive discrimination in *favour* of growth centres, but it is a plea to avoid positive discrimination *against* those centres should they emerge.

There also appears to be a good deal of misunderstanding about the role played by regional policy in determining the location of North Sea oil activities. Much of that employment is in service industries which do not attract development area assistance. In many areas the chief function of development area assistance is not to benefit new employers entering the service sector, but to assist traditional manufacturing establishments who have to adapt to a situation of extreme labour shortage by higher investment aimed at improving labour productivity. If such assistance was removed the chief result would probably be job destruction in these firms rather than job transfers between areas. There are, of course, some types of oil-related development, for example production platform activity, which does benefit from development area assistance and this may be difficult to justify, but this is often a small part of total employment.

My conclusion would be that whatever regional incentives are available, they should be available to all locations within the development area concerned. This is the position within Scotland at the moment, apart from the illogical exclusion of Edinburgh.[12] But it seems likely that the *form* of the incentives may require major modification. Despite the recent doubling of the Regional Employment Premium, regional policy in the UK remains significantly biased in favour of capital intensive development in manufacturing industry. An investigation of how we arrived at a policy which encourages capital intensive development in areas of labour surplus, and labour intensive development in areas of labour shortage, would make an interesting thesis, but it evidently owes nothing to first principles! Such a policy, carried as far as the existing system, is likely to produce a serious misallocation of resources and can be very expensive in terms of expenditure per job created. There are already clear signs that capital intensive development is being very heavily concentrated in the development areas and this might become most noticeable in Scotland in the future because many North Sea oil and gas activities are highly capital intensive by nature. For example, oil refinery and associated developments would qualify under the existing regional policy for very high investment grants. It is quite conceivable that a refining development might qualify for a grant of £100,000 per job created! There is then a strong case for reconsidering whether oil-related developments should qualify for regional policy, but there is an even stronger case for finding a new method of assistance which is more factor neutral than present policy. One method of achieving this, which I have discussed in detail elsewhere,[13] would be to vary corporation tax according to the distribution of a firm's employment between development and non-development areas.

The Distribution of Costs and Benefits: Some Implications for Local Authority Finance[14]

North Sea oil developments will require substantial capital expenditure in providing the infrastructure which is necessary to make industrial growth possible, and often this will involve authorities with very limited financial resources and bargaining powers. From this a number of important questions follow, the most important of which concerning the principles which should be applied to determine the distribution of these costs between local authorities, central government and private, commercial interests. The Shetland Bill was about this very issue as it gave the Shetland County Council quite exceptional powers to bargain with, and obtain very significant financial concessions from a number of major oil companies. But practice has run ahead of principle and we should at least consider the circumstances in which special action of this nature is relevant. I shall try to do this by considering two polar cases.

First, suppose that planning consent is given to Drumbuie (as an alternative one could substitute any production platform established in a remote area).[15] Such a decision would involve certain environmental and social costs (disruption and even demise of small communities, the loss of scenic value) and certain economic costs (loss of tourist income, the need to provide infrastructure for a project of limited duration) which would certainly be higher than those which would be incurred by the use of other sites. This is particularly true for infrastructure costs as in remote communities there is generally little spare capacity in terms of houses, roads etc. and the new investment would be likely to be seriously underused when production platform construction came to an end. The same argument would have much less force at a site such as Hunterston where less investment in infrastructure would be necessary and where there would be a strong possibility that production platform construction would be followed by other types of industrial activity.

A private firm using the Drumbuie site would therefore impose costs on the community which are likely to be substantially greater than the external costs imposed by the use of an alternative site—and this seems to have been accepted by all the expert witnesses to the Drumbuie inquiry. On the other hand, it is also agreed that the Drumbuie site would have certain unique characteristics which make it particularly suitable for production platform construction. These benefits would of course accrue to the site user. We can then formulate the principle, which is admittedly easier to formulate than to apply in practice, that the site should not be used for production platform construction unless the economic rent acquired from the use of the site is sufficient to compensate for the external costs which the use of the site impose on the community. Further, the gainer, in this case the private concern, should compensate the losers. One method of achieving this would be to estimate as far as possible the external costs imposed by the use of the site and then to auction the site subject to the condition that its sale should be sufficient to cover these extra costs.[16] Of course, such a system has very substantial imperfections in practice. How does one establish the losers? What value should be placed on the 'way of life' of small communities? What is the price of a good view? Any process of compensation must be imperfect, but this is no excuse for ignoring the principle that as far as is possible the external costs of such developments should not be borne by the community, but by the enterprises which make such developments necessary.[17]

In the Drumbuie case, and in most cases where production platform activity is concerned, the developments which impose the unwanted externalities can be fairly readily identified and the duration of the developments might be relatively short. At the other extreme we could take as a second polar case the city of Aberdeen where more than 200 new companies are involved and where the time scale of developments would appear to be substantially longer. In this case it would seem that local authorities should bear the capital costs as they will benefit over the long run through increased rateable value. The heavy capital expenditure required in the short run to make these developments possible and then be financed by borrowing.

In practice there may be considerable difficulties. First, local authorities obtain rate support grants which are equalisation grants. As rateable values increase rate support tends to diminish on virtually a one for one basis, thus transferring the costs of meeting higher capital expenditure from the central government to the occupiers of new premises. Second, to finance new construction by borrowing will, at present interest rates, bring an appreciable increase in the level of current expenditure and hence in the sums which it is necessary to raise through rates. Third, given the existing methods through which controls over capital expenditure are exercised, an increase in borrowing consents for one area is at the expense of another. Fourth, there is, except for the New Towns, no method of looking at the needs of an area as a whole as the allocation of consents is by function (roads, houses, schools etc.) and not by area. There is no doubt that the Scottish Office is acutely aware of the necessity for considerable capital expenditure by area given the particular circumstances arising from North Sea oil developments, and has already in practice made substantial efforts to adjust to the new capital expenditure needs of authorities in the Highlands and Islands and the North East of Scotland.[18] However, the whole process would merit a good deal of further study.

Some Reflections on Incomes Policy

Thus far I have considered only the possible direct impacts of North Sea oil and have taken for granted the basic decisions over licensing and taxation policy which determine the scale and the pace of such development. This simply reflects the need to draw the line somewhere. It certainly does not imply that this wider discussion is irrelevant; and to illustrate this I would like to consider one set of policy decisions relating to incomes policy which, while derived for good and pressing reasons, has proved to be quite inappropriate to the needs of areas undergoing rapid economic change. The last experiment in incomes policy is at an end, but we are quite likely to experience a new experiment in the future. If this is to be more successful and durable than the incomes policies of the past then we have to learn from our past mistakes and the rigorous application of incomes policy in the North East and Highlands and Islands of Scotland was surely one of these.

In 1971, at the beginning of North Sea oil and gas developments, both the North East and the Highlands and Islands were low wage areas.[19] The pace and scale of expansion in these areas resulted in increased competition for labour and a rapid exhaustion of the labour reserves which had been reflected in relatively higher unemployment and low activity rates. The normal market response to this would be a rise in the price of the scarce resource, in this case labour, in order to attract, through immigration, an increased supply. In addition to requiring a change in the spatial distribution of labour, a period of rapid economic change usually requires reallocation between different industries and occupations. The most obvious example in this case was the need to attract more labour into the construction industry in order to provide the additional infrastructure which immigration required.

Unfortunately none of the three phases of incomes policy allowed either of these adjustments to take place. It was not possible for established firms to raise wages relative to those paid by firms in other areas so that the general level of wages in these areas remained low. Nor was it possible for established firms in these areas to vary wage changes relative to one another. However, one category of firm was, in practice, exempt from the provisions of the policy. New firms were required to 'pay the going rate', but as the going rate could not be defined such a clause proved impossible to operate. Many firms were employing labour in occupations new to these areas. Even if this was not so it is well established that in any sizeable labour market there is a substantial wage range between the wages paid to labour for the same occupation.[20] The new firm could then set wages at whatever level was necessary to obtain the labour it required and established companies could not respond. Not surprisingly many established firms attempted to evade the policy. Some were caught, but there was no way of curbing the wages offered by incoming firms.[21]

The failure to make an allowance for a situation of rapid economic change therefore compounded inefficiency with inequity. It prevented a general rise in wages, but allowed particular firms considerable latitude. The distribution of labour which resulted was then capricious. Relaxation of the policy would not have provided any easy solution for established companies, who would have had to meet increased competition and hence higher wage costs. But such a rise is a necessary, if not sufficient condition to obtain additional labour through immigration. The other necessary condition is a rise in wages in the construction sector. It is perhaps fitting commentary on the absurdities of the incomes policy as applied that in its final phase the Pay Board was attempting to

reduce wages in eight building firms, all of whom were already short
of labour.

An unwillingness to contemplate exceptional treatment is understandable under a wage freeze period such as Phase I. However,
it is a sad reflection on our understanding of labour economics that
in Phases II and III there was still no provision which allowed any
adjustment of wage differentials to deal with labour shortages. This
was the first long-term incomes policy to make no provision for
such adjustment. Instead, criteria were developed to allow exceptional treatment in a number of circumstances where the under-
lining rationale was obscure—flexibility, unsocial hours, productivity
increases which might be quite unrelated to changes in labour
effort or working conditions etc. In a market economy these *ad hoc*
expedients are of little importance, but as long as wage flexibility
is necessary to reallocate labour, an incomes policy must allow the
wage structure to reflect fundamental changes in labour market
conditions. The most important case for exceptional treatment arises
where genuine labour shortages occur and any future, long-term
incomes policy should recognise it.

Some Concluding Remarks

As I threatened at the beginning of this paper I have wandered over
a fairly wide field without producing many final answers. This
being so, I will not attempt in this final section to provide a summary of what has come before. Rather, I will try to assess the
likely impact on North Sea oil developments on the Scottish
economy as a whole in the hope that this will provide some basis
for assessing the prospects of a major change from our depressing
economic past.

The guesses I have put forward would suggest that North Sea oil
activities might lead directly to the creation of some 25,000–30,000
additional jobs. This employment will be highly concentrated and
will certainly transform the economic prospects of certain areas. I
have attempted to stress the considerable uncertainty of these
estimates and my own view is that they are likely to err on the
conservative side: that the super-multiplier may operate rather than
the limited multiplier concept to which I have adhered in making
my calculations. There is also the prospect of acquiring an expertise
in offshore technology which can be applied in the future in areas
outside the North Sea. All of this would imply a higher level of
employment creation. On the other hand, we have to recognise that
many, indeed most, of the North Sea activities do not give rise to

permanent employment. Unless new areas are licensed, and it would be difficult to justify the case for this at the moment, exploration activity may peak in 1975 or 1976 and decline thereafter. Employment in production platform construction is likely to be at a maximum some time around 1978. Employment will increase in other directions, for example in production and in refining, but for the most part such employment is likely to arise in areas which are different from those mainly affected by exploration and production platform activity. Hence, particular communities might be subject to large fluctuations in employment. This is particularly likely in the Highlands and Islands and the problem is aggravated by the fact that the employment creation is large relative to the communities affected who will then have great difficulty in adapting to any subsequent decline. We should not conclude from this that such development should be resisted in all circumstances, for temporary employment is better than continued unemployment and may leave behind some more permanent benefits in the terms of a better infrastructure, capable of sustaining faster growth in the future. Nonetheless, we must be aware of these difficulties if we are to meet them in the future.

We have seen that North Sea oil and gas will have a substantial impact on certain communities and some of these will continue to benefit for a considerable period in the future. However, these lie outside the industrial heartland of the country, and in particular are removed from the Clydeside area which is the focus of the greatest social and economic problems. It is therefore quite possible that the direct impact from North Sea oil will still leave Clydeside, and hence the Scottish economy as a whole, with the familiar problems of low incomes, high unemployment and high emigration. On this there is plenty of scope for disagreement, but my own view would be that the direct impact of North Sea oil and gas offers too narrow and restricted an industrial base to transform the prospects for the whole of the Scottish economy. The magnitude of this task is formidable. The estimate of primary North Sea job creation of 25,000–30,000 has its limitations, but, even if we bear these in mind, we have to set these estimates against a known rate of job loss in the primary, extractive and manufacturing sectors in Scotland which amounted to no less than *26,000 jobs per annum* over 1966–72, a period in which Scotland did relatively well compared to her economic performance in the 1950s and early 1960s.

Hence, while the direct impact of North Sea oil will be important in providing a new and significant growth sector something more will be needed. This is where we enter the realm of political economy. As I emphasised at the beginning of this paper the indirect effects of North Sea oil on the balance of payments and on government revenue will be quantitatively much more important than the direct effects impinging on the Scottish economy. This is now implicitly recognised by all the major political parties who are committed to establishing a development agency, financed by a share of the revenue of North Sea oil, which will attempt to promote faster economic and industrial development in Scotland. While the direct impacts loom largest at the moment, such an agency may well prove more important in the future. If so, we may see, at long last, a major sea-change in Scotland's economic performance—it is, indeed, long overdue.

Notes

1. Peak production will probably last only some three years in each of these fields and may decline subsequently by some 10 per cent per annum.
2. Department of Energy, *Production and Reserves of Oil and Gas in the UK*, HMSO, 1974.
3. Department of Energy, *United Kingdom Offshore Oil and Gas Policy*, HMSO, 1974.
4. For a more detailed discussion of the classification adopted see, M. Gaskin, 'The Economic Impact of North Sea Oil in Scotland', *Three Banks Review*, March 1973.
5. International Management and Engineering Group of Britain Ltd., *Study of Potential Benefits to British Industry from Offshore Oil and Gas Developments*, HMSO, 1972. The level of expenditure will be significantly higher than IMEG estimated but the proportion accounted for production platform construction may be reasonably accurate.
6. I base this observation on the expectation that exploration activity will peak sometime in 1975–6 and production platform activity sometime in 1976–7.
7. Taking a long-run employment multiplier of the size which appears to be suggested by A. J. Brown, *The Framework of Regional Economics in the United Kingdom*, 1972.
8. John Hicks, *The Trade Cycle*, p. 62.
9. T. Wilson 'The Regional Multiplier—A Critique', *Oxford Economic Papers*, MS 20, 1968.
10. 4,400 out of the present employment of 4,545 in the North East and 3,370 out of the forecast increase of 3,690 in the North East.
11. See, N. Trimble, 'Estimated Demand for Supply Boat Berths in Scotland, 1974–80', North Sea Study Group, Department of Political Economy, Occasional Paper No. 2, January 1945.
12. This exclusion still applied at the date of completing the original paper (29 July 1974). Edinburgh was granted full development status in August. I have let the original statement stand as a monument to my perspicacity!
13. D. I. Mackay, *A New Approach to Regional Policy*, Poland Street Paper No. 1, 1973.

14. Some of the ideas in the following section have been suggested to me by Diane Dawson of the Department of Political Economy, University of Glasgow.
15. Of course, after the completion of this paper planning consent for Drumbuie was refused by the Secretary of State for Scotland. I have let the argument stand as the principles on which it was based still apply.
16. This course would be made more difficult by the fact that the existing law of compulsory purchase forces a local authority to pay development value and not value in current use. Evidently, this would leave the local authority little scope for profit through auctioning the site between competitive bidders.
17. The basic principles underlying this argument are in no way affected by the decision to nationalise future production platform sites and then rent them to subsequent users. Thus, the annual rent should vary from site to site according to the external costs imposed on the community. Renting also offers the possibility of achieving a better match between appropriate platform design and site usage.
18. For a clear description of what has already been done to assist these authorities to adapt to new demands see Dr. G. McCrone, 'The Role of Central and Local Authorities', *The Institute of Petroleum Conference*, Aviemore, May 1974.
19. Average hourly male manual earnings in the Highlands and Islands were 93 per cent of the Scottish average and 90 per cent of the British average. The corresponding figures for the North East were 89 per cent and 87 per cent. See, *New Earnings Survey*, 1971, HMSO p. 133.
20. D. I. Mackay, *et al.*, *Labour Markets Under Different Employment Conditions*, 1972 and D. Robinson, *Wage Drift, Fringe Benefits and Manpower Distribution*, OECD, 1968.
21. The Pay Board found 'widespread' infringement of the code by established firms in the Aberdeen area. (First Report, p. 6) and 'in contrast to the allegations, infringements occurred almost exclusively in established firms'. This, of course, was possibly what the 'allegations' predicted. New firms in setting their initial wage level were *not* restrained by this code. Naturally, they found it easier to abide by the code thereafter!

11

Economic Growth in Scotland: Theory and Experience

David Simpson[*]

The scope of this paper stretches from the beginning of the eighteenth century to the present day. The reason for taking such a large sweep of history is that, contrary to the modern view, I believe that economic growth can only be understood in historical perspective. At the beginning of the period under consideration Scotland had not yet begun her industrialisation, nor had she entered into the incorporating political union with England, perhaps the two most important features of the recent history of the country. Today we seem about to enter a new phase of economic and political change.

Given the scope of the topic, a paper of reasonable size must evidently be severely selective. I shall concentrate on what I take to be the salient characteristics of economic growth in Scotland over the last two-and-a-half centuries, recognising quite frankly that the choice of such features is subjective and open to debate. After a short outline of the period the paper opens with an account of these characteristics. This is followed by the presentation of a theory of economic growth. Considerations of space preclude a survey of all possible growth theories to show whether or not they fit the 'stylised' facts better. Readers may judge for themselves whether or not the chosen theory offers an adequate explanation.[1] Finally, some implications are drawn for economic policy.

Campbell[2] has divided the course of events since 1700 into three phases or periods. Phase I covers the years up to about 1780. In this period, Scotland was still an agrarian and trading economy,

[*] Director of the Fraser of Allander Institute for Research on the Scottish Economy at the University of Strathclyde. Readers of this paper who have some acquaintance with Scottish economic history will recognise the debt which I owe to Professor Roy Campbell. My slight knowledge of the period is based almost entirely on his published works. Needless to say he can in no way be blamed for the interpretation I have placed on his account of events.

but it is possible to detect, with hindsight, signs of the foundations being laid for the period of industrial growth which followed. Led by the cotton, and later the iron industries, Phase II, a period of industrial expansion, lasted from about 1780 to about 1870. At this time Scotland was pre-eminent in a number of industrial activities, but the following period, Phase III, from about 1870 to the present day was marked by industrial decline. Campbell points out that the symptoms of decline tended to be concealed until about 1914 by the progress of the steel and shipbuilding industries. Thus, in this view, the Scottish economy has described a full circle from relative backwardness in 1700 through international pre-eminence to relative backwardness once again in the middle of the twentieth century. This paper is not concerned with questions of the timing of the cycle. But we shall devote particular attention to one sub-phase of Phase III, namely the thirty-year period since the Second World War.

The Stylised Facts

There are six characteristic features of the process to which I should like to draw attention. Although they can be equally well identified in other countries and other time periods, I propose to discuss them largely in the context of Scotland since 1700. The first concerns the *relative rate of growth of output.* Next to the change in the absolute rate of growth of output, associated in most countries with industrialisation, perhaps the most striking of all economic observations[3] are the differences *between countries* in their rates of growth during any given period of time. So far as Scotland is concerned, we have of course no historical series of national income estimates which would allow an exact comparison with the experience of other countries. But for the purposes of this paper I may perhaps be permitted to take it as a 'stylised fact' that from 1700 to 1870 (i.e. during Campbell's Phases I and II), the rate of economic growth in Scotland increased with respect to England and other leading Western European countries,[4] while thereafter it fell.

   The second feature of economic growth to which I would like to draw attention is the effect of economic growth on *the personal distribution of income.* Again we have no hard facts to rely on, but I would suggest that the overall impression conveyed by Scottish pieces of evidence is that the personal distribution of income became less equal during the phases of expansion (Phases I and II) and more equal during the phase of decline (Phase III).[5] What I am proposing then as another stylised fact to be explained is that the rate of economic growth varies inversely with the equality of the personal distribution of income.

The third feature of economic growth which strikes me as being particularly significant is what may be called *accessibility to markets*. It is commonplace that the Act of Union gave Scottish producers access to markets in the English colonies, although the connection with Scotland's later industrialisation is not so direct as is commonly supposed. Less well-known perhaps is the frequency with which the fortunes of particular industries have been affected by the chance loss or gain of markets.

Changing market accessibility may be closely related to the fourth characteristic of the process of economic growth on which we wish to focus attention. This is the process of *specialisation*. It is entirely appropriate that we should illustrate what we mean by specialisation by drawing on an example from the *Wealth of Nations*,[6] particularly as the passage contains a very vivid account of a typical lowlands farm in seventeenth-century Scotland.

According to Smith, the increased price realised by Scottish cattle exported to England following the Union[7] made it profitable to devote land to cultivation in order to raise food for cattle. Previously, food for human consumption was grown on the small area of tilled land, while cattle were grazed on the abundant un-improved land. Hence the increasing demand for meat caused an increase in the degree of 'roundaboutness' of production. Formerly, meat was produced by feeding cattle on unimproved pasture: the new activity of cultivating land in order to produce cattle fodder represents a new step in the process of specialisation. This process has continued until today we give the name 'Agribusiness' to the complex of activities and the several industries which have been created by the process of specialisation. Thus the significance of specialisation in the process of economic growth is the diversification of economic activities, not the steady expansion of the level of output of a given set of activities. What evidence is there that specialisation in this sense has been a characteristic feature of economic growth in Scotland since 1700? The nature of the process is such that general statistical evidence would be difficult to collect: it is certainly not available. Again, one must rely on scattered and impressionistic evidence in asking the reader to accept specialisation as another stylised fact.

The fifth feature of Scottish economic growth has been the presence of some coherent direction or leadership during the expansionary phases. In Phase I leadership was provided by ele-ments of the landed aristocracy who combined ownership of land with technical knowledge and a concern for improvement in the

L

widest sense. In Phase II leadership passed into the hands of middle-class owners of family firms—living examples of the text-book entrepreneur. During Phase III, their influence waned as the family firm has given way to the private or public corporation, whose organisation and motives have been so elegantly dissected by Galbraith. The absence of leadership has certainly been a notable feature of the declining phase of the Scottish economy since 1870.

Natural resources are the sixth and last characteristic feature of the growth process which I should like to emphasise. Their signifi-cance for growth in other countries has been widely debated, but their role in the Scottish context is undeniable. The discovery and ultimately the exhaustion of deposits of cheap iron-ore and coal were a key feature of industrialisation in nineteenth-century Scot-land.

We have identified then six features of the process of economic growth in Scotland: the unequal (compared to other countries) rate of growth, the changing distribution of income, the influence of changes in market accessibility, specialisation, leadership and natu-ral resources. Natural resources need no explanation. What expla-nation can be offered for the other phenomena?

A Classical Theory of Economic Growth

Almost fifty years ago the American economist Allyn Young delivered a Presidential address to Section F of the British Associa-tion meeting in Glasgow. Three months later his paper was pub-lished in the *Economic Journal* (December 1928, Vol. 38 No. 152). If Economics possessed a citation index, as do the natural sciences, this article would surely prove to be among the most frequently cited. Yet, scanning the contemporary literature on the theory of economic growth, its influence would appear to be non-existent. A footnote usually acknowledges the article as a deviation from the mainstream of thinking about economic growth. In his paper 'Increasing Returns and Economic Progress', Young set out to give a restatement of Adam Smith's theory of economic growth,[8] founded on his concept of the division of labour. He described Smith's dictum that 'the division of labour is limited by the extent of the market'[9] as being 'the most illuminating and fruitful generalisation found anywhere in the whole literature of economics'.[10]

Young recalled that Adam Smith saw that the division of labour transformed a group of complex processes into a succession of simpler processes which lend themselves to the use of machinery. According to Young, the division of labour induces not just organisational change *but the introduction of new technology and its embodiment in new capital goods* (which is to say the using of labour in roundabout or indirect ways). Such technical progress leads to an increase in the volume of production, in income generated and thus to increases in the size of the market. 'Thus change becomes progressive and propagates itself in accumulative way.'[11] To this theory of growth, Young attached the title 'Increasing Returns'.

This elementary classical theory of economic growth has been overlooked perhaps because it cannot usefully be formulated in terms of the familiar neo-classical analysis.[12] First of all, it is not an equilibrium analysis. Thus the textbook treatment of the case of increasing returns to scale is concerned with the behaviour of costs and prices in an individual firm or industry. The product, the firm, and its operations, other than the level of output, are taken to be unchanged throughout the analysis. The neo-classical analysis of the theory of value therefore relegates to the field of external economies the forces which are central to Smith's theory of economic growth. Again, we are accustomed to representing changes in scale by continuous changes in the level of output. But Schumpeter has pointed out that *discontinuities* are the characteritic features of growth. 'It is not the *level* of operation of a given degree of roundaboutness which matters, but the act of introducing it.'[13] The neo-classical theory of growth is essentially a theory of the adjustment towards a new equilibrium arising from some exogenous disturbance of the old equilibrium. The classical theory, on the other hand, is a theory of disturbances many of which are engendered from within the economic system itself.[14]

To attempt a refinement or formalisation of this classical model of growth would take us far from the main task of the paper, which is to examine to what extent it offers an explanation of the five characteristic features of economic growth in Scotland.

The observed disparity of growth rates between regions has been investigated by Myrdal.[15] He invoked what he called a process of cumulative causation to explain it. This process is in fact similiar to that which Young describes as increasing returns. It is easy to see that with increasing returns, the opening of trade between two regions may aggravate and not diminish the difference in comparative costs between them. So one region may benefit at the expense of another, in contrast to the conventional neo-classical analysis where the opening of trade must benefit both regions[16] (although not necessarily equally). So our theory is quite consistent with the observed disparities in regional growth rates. While tariff barriers between Scotland and England had been removed in 1707, high transport costs acted as effective protection for Scottish manufacturers against English competition until the completion of cross-border railway links in 1850. The Scottish metal industries continued to enjoy the cost advantages conferred by their proximity to high quality ore deposits until these were exhausted twenty years later, about 1870. From about that time may be traced the apparent decline in the rate of growth of the Scottish economy with respect to England.

We can invoke the same principle of cumulative causation or increasing returns to account for the disequalisation of the personal distribution of income. The same social and economic forces engendered in the process of growth which lead to a less equal distribution of income between regions operate to increase income inequality among persons. Those who, at the beginning of the process, are less well-endowed suffer at the expense of those who are better-endowed initially. If one performs the intellectual experiment of letting any society follow a policy of maximum growth without regard to social costs, it seems certain that the result would be a distribution of income which was highly unequal both with regard to persons and to regions. Conversely, institutions and policies which are designed to shield less well-endowed persons and regions from these costs can only operate as a brake on the mechanism of growth.

The third and fourth features to which we draw attention, viz. access to markets and specialisation are of course an integral part of our growth theory. Degree of specialisation, or division of labour, is limited by the extent of the market, and the size of the market in turn is governed by the degree of specialisation.

Where does our fifth feature, leadership, fit into the theory? The answer is quite simple. A change in the degree of specialisation, with the associated technical progress, cannot take place automatically. Such changes require organisation by some human agency—it is difficult to imagine that this decision-making function could ever be automated. The precise human agency will vary according to the historical period. In Phase I it was the landed classes (more specifically, the Lowland landed class), in Phase II and the early part of III it has been the entrepreneurs. In the latter part of Phase III the entrepreneur has ceased to play his traditional role. The emigration of the mobile factors of production, capital and skilled labour from the lagging to the relatively faster growing region is a significant feature of Myrdal's model. And there can be little doubt that there has been a continuing even accelerating, net outflow of private capital and skilled labour, especially those with entrepreneurial skills, from Scotland to England since the last quarter of the nineteenth century.

Much of the foregoing analysis is commonplace, but it seems necessary to establish both a working theory and a historical perpective if we are to understand events and to judge economic policy in Scotland since the Second World War.

The Economy in Decline

The relative decline of the Scottish economy can be traced back to he period beginning in the 1870s. Up to that time a successful base had been established of iron and heavy engineering. These industries had gone through a sequence of organisational and technical change which can plausibly be summarised by our classical theory of growth. It would have been perfectly natural, then, to expect that the sequence of industrial progress would be continued by the evolution of new industries as the older ones declined. But this did not happen. In some cases ventures did begin and then failed (motor vehicles and aircraft), in others there were few attempts to keep pace with scientific progress in other countries (chemicals), while significantly many new industries were begun under foreign (mainly American) leadership (rubber, sewing-machines). This last development is surely indicative of a serious failure of indigenous entrepreneurship. This is supported by the fragmentary evidence of a very low level of private investment in industry in Scotland, at least in the twentieth century. In the last quarter of the nineteenth century the traditional family firm was already giving way through mergers and takeovers to the joint-stock company. Whether this was the reason for the collapse of Scottish entrepreneurship or not it does seem to have collapsed, with predictable consequences for Scottish economic growth.

It might be expected that, following this abandonment of responsibility by the capitalist class in Scotland as the twentieth century moved on, economic leadership would pass into new hands. And, indeed, after the Second World War, the British Government accepted responsibility for maintaining full employment in Britain. But so far as economic growth in Scotland was concerned, this commitment fell short of what was required in two critical respects. First, it was not envisaged by any sector of opinion that the Government should take over the organisational or leadership role abandoned by the capitalists.[17] It was regarded as sufficient that the Government should confine itself to regulating the aggregate level of effective demand through monetary and fiscal instruments. The Government operated on the demand side of the economy, whereas what was required to get the growth process under way was organi-

sational efforts on the supply side. The second difficulty was that
government policy was never directed towards the promotion of a
process of self-sustaining economic growth in Scotland. The policy
adopted was one of the alleviation of unemployment.[18] While it
actually originated in the late 1930s and underwent many changes
of form, this policy has come to be known as 'Regional Policy'.
Ironically, Scottish unemployment levels relative to England since
Regional Policy has been in force have been worse than before the
war. It is not our purpose in this paper[19] to analyse the reasons for
the failure of this policy. Instead we conclude by considering the
ingredients of a successful policy of economic growth which may be
suggested by the theory we have discussed.

Towards a Policy for Economic Growth in Scotland

Let us consider, in reverse order, each of the five elements of the
growth process which are under policy control. First of all comes
the question of leadership. Few would dispute that, in the present
period of history, leadership in a strategy of economic growth can
only come from Government: there are simply no other contenders.

Leadership
The first essential element in the execution of any policy is political
will. It is difficult to see a central government having the necessary
political will to carry out in a single region a policy of economic
growth, as distinct from a policy of regional compensation. A growth
policy would meet competing, perhaps even conflicting, interests
from other regions. Political support would, at the very best, be
lukewarm. No such inhibitions would be felt by a sovereign government in the region concerned. Secondly, sovereign regions can adopt
a wide range of policy instruments including measures which are not
open to non-sovereign regions. Because of the range and diversity
of its activities in a modern economy, a sovereign government can act
as a catalyst or, to use a different metaphor, as a pole of growth to
stimulate the growth process in a lagging region.

While the scope of government at this strategic level is clear and
uncontroversial, at a lower level of economic organisation the form
of government intervention is neither. Many solutions have been
canvassed. I have no specific solution to urge, but I would suggest
that we should not shrink from treating institutions as instrument
variables. Thus, it may be that some form of worker responsibility
is an essential ingredient of any framework for sustained growth in
this period of history, and that institutional forms of productive

organisations must be altered accordingly. Such changes would at the same time seem to be consistent with a successful anti-inflationary policy. However, this is only an illustration. The important thing I wish to emphasise is the classical principle of institutions as endogenous variables in the growth process, as opposed to the neo-classical view that they are exogenous.

Specialisation

Changes in the degree of specialisation—which are the essence of the growth process—tend to take place in the region where production is initially located. If a branch factory is set up in another region, then, while the level of output might be varied at that new location, a further step in the process of specialisation is unlikely to take place there. Thus we have the familiar problem of the branch factory economy. The structure of incentives laid down by Regional Policy in postwar Scotland has tended to discriminate in favour of branch factories, and against indigenous enterprises. A policy of economic growth would presumably seek to do the reverse.

Access to Markets

There are limits to the extent to which a small country can control its own economy if it wishes to benefit from the international division of labour. To protect itself against the vagaries of world market conditions a small country needs to follow an export policy of market diversification and product differentiation. If these principles of export policy are followed, then most protectionist barriers in world markets can be hurdled, and there is no need to join one protectionist bloc or another. Switzerland and the Scandanavian countries afford examples of small countries operating successfully in world markets with relatively low tariffs themselves. In the event of some catastrophic simultaneous cutting-off of all world markets, a necessary insurance policy is to have the potential resource capacity for domestic substitution of imported essential primary products. Scotland appears to be well-placed in this respect.

Distribution of Regional and Personal Incomes

These last two characteristics are of course rather symptoms of economic growth than causes. If our previous arguments are correct, it will follow that a successful growth policy in Scotland will set up tendencies towards more inequality in the distribution of income amongst persons and amongst regions within Scotland. These are problems which we shall have to learn to cope with.

Conclusions

We have discussed so far those factors influencing economic growth which are within our control. If we can get these right, then this is the most we can do. So far as natural resources are concerned, the outlook is hopeful. The change in the world terms of trade in favour of primary products must benefit our natural resource endowment of land, oil, deep water, fresh water, and fresh air, resources regarded for so long as either worthless or non-existent. If, as the classical economists speculated, this change represents a long-run tendency, then the prospects must be strong that the 1970s will mark a turning point in which Scotland enters a new phase in its economic history. In this phase its rate of growth will increase relative to that of England and other countries of Western Europe.

Notes

1. I do not mean to imply that there necessarily exists any single theory offering a complete explanation of the historical facts.
2. R. H. Campbell, *Scotland Since 1707*, Oxford, 1971.
3. See T. A. Haavelmo, *The Theory of Economic Evolution*, Amsterdam, 1954.
4. In this connection, it does not seem to me to matter very much whether Scotland is regarded as a region or a nation, since I suppose that any satisfactory explanation of inter-regional differences in economic growth should also account for international differences.
5. See, for example, L. Soltow, 'An Index of the Poor and the Rich of Scotland', *Scottish Journal of Political Economy*, February 1971.
6. A. Smith, 'Wealth of Nations' (Cannan ed.), New York, 1937, pp. 220–2.
7. Smith does not say why the Union should have raised the price, since cattle were being exported to England without restriction before the Union. In a private communication, Professor Campbell has suggested that the rising demand for beef by the Navy in the eighteenth century may be the explanation.
8. Not to be confused with the 'growth model' attributed to Smith by Hicks in Chapter 4 of *Capital and Growth*. As Hicks acknowledges (p. 38), this is not a growth model at all.
9. Smith, op. cit., p. 17.
10. A Young, op. cit., p. 529.
11. A. Young, op. cit., p. 533.
12. Since the neo-classical analysis springs from the theory of value it is not necessarily the most appropriate framework for studying economic growth.
13. J. Schumpeter, 'The Instability of Capitalism', *Economic Journal*, September 1928. See also his remark 'Industrial discontinuities (are) the carriers of essential phenomena', op. cit., p. 382.

14. It is the unsettling nature of progress which arouses so much opposition to it.
15. G. Myrdal, *Economic Theory and Underdeveloped Regions*, London, 1957.
16. For a more detailed discussion, see N. Kaldor, 'The Case for Regional Policies', *Scottish Journal of Political Economy*, November, 1970.
17. Of those who advocated the public ownership of *all* the means of production, few had any coherent strategy of economic growth in mind.
18. Campbell, op. cit., pp. 319–26, Kaldor, op. cit.
19. The author is writing a paper on this topic which he hopes may be published shortly.

12

Administering Scotland: a Critique and Forward Look

*James G. Kellas**

When Professor Alexander suggested the title 'administering Scotland' to me, I think he had in mind what most economists like to think of as the proper position of politics in the running of a country: the administration of master plans made up by economists. I accepted the title, not so much because I agreed with the implied pecking order as between politics and economics, but because it was a peculiarly apt description of the position of Scotland in the Government of the United Kingdom. Scotland is 'administered' rather than 'governed', because its political system is essentially defective and anomalous.

There are many things that are separate in Scotland: the presbyterian Church of Scotland, the system of Scots Law, and the school system, and to a large extent they run their own affairs from Edinburgh.

But despite the existence of the Scottish Office, and the Scottish Grand Committee in the House of Commons, the government of Scotland must fall into line with the government of Great Britain (and Northern Ireland), because there is no government of Scotland at all owing its existence to a vote of the Scottish people. People do vote in Scotland, of course, but the MPs they elect sit in the House of Commons, and it does not matter what the majority is from Scotland—the largest number in the House of Commons as a whole forms the Government, and that Government governs Scotland. How it *administers* Scotland is another matter, for Scotland is a difficult place to run from a distance. Hence the 10,000 or so Scottish Office civil servants and the ever-increasing field stations of the UK Departments. The crunch comes when administration on a territorial basis becomes a sort of government on its own—independent of HQ. This is what Whitehall and Westminster have naturally

* Senior Lecturer in Politics, University of Glasgow

resisted ever since James VI and I left Edinburgh for London in 1603, but which is probably about to take place through the actions of the voters in the February 1974 election.

Make no mistake about it, the slaughter of the 'two-party' vote in Scotland (that is, the vote for the Labour and Conservative parties) in February, brought that very curious document, the Kilbrandon Report on the Constitution, back on to the bookshop shelves from the basements to which it was speedily being confined. Thirty per cent of the Scottish voters deserted the major parties at the election (much more than the Liberals' 21 per cent in England) —and 22 per cent of these went to the SNP. Devolution could no longer be ignored, and 'administering Scotland' was much more difficult for London.

And just in time too, from any political standpoint, when one knows a bit more about the political and economic problems of Scotland. For the first and last problem for Scotland is how to communicate its needs to those in a position to act and then to get action. There is no hostility to Scotland in London among the powers that be, but there is great ignorance and bewilderment. This is as much the fault of the Scots as of the metropolitans. For many years they have kept themselves to themselves, and have tried not to make a nuisance in the affairs of state. They have not thrown bombs, defied the Crown, or fought on the wrong side during the wars. They have admired the party leaders (at least as much as anyone has) and taken jobs in their governments, parliaments and civil services. All they asked in return was equality and respect.

On the whole they got it, and it is perfectly reasonable to congratulate the British political system as it applied to Scotland and Wales (unfortunately not to Ireland) for being tolerant of national differences, and moreover profitable to the pocket. There was certainly a time when many advanced thinkers would have done away with all the relics of Scotland's political independence in the name of British citizenship and progress.

Why not now? I return to the problem of administering Scotland and the communication of its needs to London. It has become clear in the last fifteen years or so—and especially in the last three because of oil—that economic circumstances in Scotland have put a peculiar strain on the tradition of just administering UK policies in Scotland through the Scottish Office and the field stations of the other departments. All through the 1960s, the economic planning of Britain was based on the Whitehall view that regional development was subservient to the needs of the UK economy as a whole, and that it was no use, for example, propping up an industry in Scotland just for the sake of the economy of Scotland. It had to be sensible

for the running of that industry as a whole in Britain. Thus the steel
industry (now nationalised) ceased to operate on a regional basis,
but became organised by products.

Similarly, fiscal policies were based on the needs of the British
economy, not the Scottish economy, with deflationary measures for
'over-heating'—something which applied to the south and Midlands
of England but not to Scotland. A similar situation arose recently
with blanket wage restrictions under Phase III penalising local firms
in the oil areas, who cannot compete with the high wages offered by
the oil companies.

The Scottish Office, who presumably know better, are in no
position to challenge Whitehall on economic policy. This is because
the function of the Scottish Office in economic matters has always
been to 'administer' rather than to formulate policy. It does of
course put pressure on Whitehall to change that policy in the interests of Scotland, but there can never be a 'Scottish' economic policy
from Whitehall. A 'regional' policy, perhaps. But not a Scottish
policy.

Hence the dilemma of the Scottish Office. It exists to administer
Scotland (and only Scotland). Its vision is Scotland, and its successes
and failures are in Scotland. But it administers policies which have
a British vision, and whose successes and failures are chalked up on
the British political score-board.

The interesting thing here is that until quite recently there was
no obvious contradiction between Scottish and British requirements.
The old-style Scottish Office did not trouble itself at all with economic policy as such. It looked after social policy (especially the
educational system and the Health Service), and the affairs of local
government (notably housing and town and country planning). But
in the 1940s and 1950s it got involved in electricity, roads and
transport, which soon led it to consider what the economy of Scotland was doing. By 1963 it felt confident enough to issue the
Central Scotland Plan, followed by the plan for Scotland as a whole
in 1966.

But even then, no contradictions between Scottish and British
requirements were mentioned. Time and time again it was said by
Scottish Office planners that if only the British economy was in
order, Scotland would be taken care of, and 'administration' of
British policies in Scotland would suffice.

It should be said that economists, politicians and administrators
concurred in this view, at least until the late 1960s, and perhaps
early 1970s. Moreover, the publication of a Scottish Budget by the
Treasury in 1969 (to refute SNP arguments) indicated that money
was coming into Scotland from the Exchequer at a greater rate than

it was being returned in taxes. It would not be rational to cut Scotland off from the benefits of Whitehall largesse, or to question the wisdom of an all-British fiscal policy.

I think opinion started to shift just before the oil bonanza made conversions on the scale of a Billy Graham Crusade. It is of course easy for anyone with the benefits of hindsight to say that such-and-such was leading inevitably to a certain result. The SNP successes of 1967–8 led many commentators to say that the SNP would win a majority of seats at the next election. In the event, they won only a single seat. As far as voting is concerned, we must still be wary of jumping on the SNP band-wagon a second time, at least in academic terms. Voters are very fickle these days, and political scientists have shared some of the opprobrium heaped on the opinion polls for failing to do the impossible: to predict certainty in a situation of flux.

But the SNP apart (although this is highly hypothetical), I think that the administration of Scotland was bound to change in the 1970s. As I indicated before, the Scottish Office got into economic planning in 1963 before nationalism was really a force, and was certainly independent of it. It hired economists, and began to think in terms of what Sir Alex Cairncross called 'The Scottish Economy'. This was the equivalent to the vision of the Scots lawyers, teachers and ministers, who had kept the Scottish nation alive since 1707.

From this there seems to be no going back, and oil has merely been the ignition of a flame which Whitehall cannot ignore. For the tables are truly turned, when the Scottish economy fires the British and not the other way round. But I regret to say that so far the Scottish Office has not grasped its oil opportunities with both hands: Whitehall has kept the initiative.

But I have jumped ahead a little. Before oil there were tremendous reappraisals in Scotland about 'identity'. In the nineteenth century, Scotland was thought of as 'North Britain', especially by the Scots, who wanted the English to accept them as equal citizens, speaking the same language and occupying the same jobs with the same salaries. Today, there is no talk of North Britain, but there is a big divide between those who want to assert 'Scottishness' and those who put British or European considerations first. In the middle, there are those who take a pragmatic approach—and here I think a large number of floating voters are to be found—they judge the effectiveness of using a Scottish or British catchphrase (whether it be 'Scotland's Oil' or 'British sovereignty') according to the pay-off in government attention to their own interests. This is what unites the SNP people with the TUC: parochial self-interest.

So 'identity' is in part self-interest. But the debate moved on a higher plane than that at times. The Kilbrandon Report on the

Constitution asked a lot of people in Scotland (and elsewhere) who they thought they were, and what a nation was. The Commissioners were no doubt a little surprised at the strength of national feeling in Scotland, though they noted that nearly all the people in established positions of authority wanted to retain the status quo. But they could not ignore the illogical structure of the Scottish political system—a legal branch, an administrative branch, but no legislative or executive branches. Curiously, they had to point these illogicalities out to many Scots before they too wondered what kind of a set-up they were living under, and whether it could not be improved.

The debate on identity was also pushed along by the Wheatley Report on local government reform. Unlike the Commission on the Constitution, this was the result of bureaucratic initiative, not grassroots electoral disturbance. Local government reform was to be centralising not decentralising, and although Scotland was to be different from England no one expected any kind of 'home rule' on a nation-wide basis. Indeed, it was precisely the lack of a Scottish dimension in the new system which worried some people—coupled with the fantastic size of the new regional authorities. Strathclyde ($2\frac{1}{2}$ millions) and the Highlands (half the area of Scotland) now appeared as local democracies, but Scotland as a whole did not. Yet without all-Scottish planning of roads, power and industrial development the new regions meant nothing. Wheatley could not consider that—it was not 'local' government, nor could the planners in Edinburgh be brought into a system of representative government.

There were many other side-shows on the road to the great Scottish reappraisal of identity, and they are still cropping up daily. UCS in 1971, with Jimmy Reid's communist nationalism; the Hunterston dream, with the BSC's snub to the Scottish plan for a multimillion steel works; Drumbuie and the late Tory Government's threat to suspend all Scottish inquiries into oil-related developments, in the British interest; the proclaiming of London as oil capital of the world by the insensitive (or English nationalist) Peter Emery in the same Government. Both major parties are trying to undo some of this, by diverting funds and civil servants to Scotland, but it is probably too late. The debate on identity is practically concluded, with the British-identifiers in retreat.

If I may return to the economists, in conclusion, I could suggest that the science of economics has proved no more stable or reliable in the debate about change in the Scottish context than has the less rigorous science of politics. Throughout the 1960s, when nationalism and devolution were being discussed, the vast majority of economists gave forth the view that it would be a bad thing to tamper with the existing machinery of government. With perhaps a less than satisfactory knowledge of political science to back them up, the economists tried to demonstrate how futile it was to introduce devolution or federal arrangements in Britain when the central government would be apparently subsidising the regional governments. All this, they said, would merely leave power where it was already—at the centre—and make the peripheral areas poorer off.

But this is to ignore the political aspects of economic policy— already demonstrated this year by the effects of the 1974 elections, though fairly muted; and the experience of decentralised political systems such as Canada, Australia, the United States and West Germany, all of whom contrive to share power and resources between the centre and the provinces. It is no accident that economic resources are given to the regions of a country where political pressure is mobilised, and where institutions exist of a regional character to bargain with the central government.

Few economists in Scotland today argue against devolution or even independence—at least with the vigour of the 1960s. It is difficult to produce economic theories which deny that with total independence and control over oil, Scotland would gain financially. And the need to keep the 'British economy' intact looks less attractive now than ever before. Devolution is also considered respectable, if it has 'teeth' (i.e. economic powers, with some sort of a share of oil revenues).

The emergence of a new-Texas or a new-Alberta in Scotland ought to turn our attention to the old Texas and the old Alberta, both significantly to be found in federal states. Texas and Alberta have kept a good share of their oil wealth, so that very little is given to or taken from the federal government in taxation and grants. Yet they are both integral parts of their respective countries.

There may be many things which Scotland would not wish to copy from Texas or Alberta, but we should at least recognise that they have grappled with the problem of self-government and the politics of oil in a federal system, a type of government to which many in Scotland now aspire (though conservatism prevents the name being used). Because of this combination of political and economic features which are relevant to Scotland, perhaps we should spend less time looking to Norway for inspiration, and spend a little more time finding out what Alberta and Texas have made of their political economy. But because of the special nature of Scottish nationalism, change is bound to be 'in the Scottish context'.

Economics and the Arts

M

13

The Economics of Cultural Subsidy

*Nick Baigent**

The purpose of this paper is to examine some arguments for subsidising the Arts in the light of welfare economics. A complete
consideration of the justification of subsidies would draw on knowledge from a wider field. But economists should be able to contribute
usefully because the Arts use resources in the form of skilled
manpower and buildings that could be put to alternative uses. If
subsidies increase the allocation of resources to the Arts, other
output is foregone compared with the allocation that would result
from freely operating markets. Optimal resource allocation lies at
the heart of welfare economics.

The economist's approach is based on the fundamental theorem
of welfare economics; a competitive system of markets will allocate
resources in a Pareto optimal way as long as there are no public
goods, externalities or increasing returns. 'Pareto optimal' refers to
the highly desirable property of not being able to make anyone
better off without at the same time making others worse off. Public
goods and externalities refer to effects which are not bought or
sold; (e.g. defence, pollution). Increasing returns causes the unit
cost of an activity to fall as output is increased. The approach of
welfare economics is to identify the presence of market failure and
recommend policies which restore the system to a Pareto optimum.
Intuitively we wish all activities to be increased to the point at which
any further increase does not yield benefits large enough to cover
the cost to society as a whole; for the Arts, is this point reached by
a free market or would a subsidy yield advantages greater than the
output foregone of other activities, as a result of the subsidy?

It is useful to begin with a point of view that is often expressed
in 'practical' politics: the Arts are a good thing and ought to be

* Lecturer in Economics, University of Reading. This article is considerably
  abridged from its original form.

supported. The obvious shortcoming of this argument is that it may well be a necessary condition in some sense for public support of the Arts, but it is nowhere near sufficient. By increasing the allocation of resources to the Arts consumers are deprived of the alternative output of these resources. The argument just given fails to explain the basis of valuing an increase in culture greater than what consumers would have preferred to consume had they freely chosen. In particular whose values are being set over the values of ordinary consumers?

A second argument that fails is associated with the Baumol-Bowen thesis[1] that the technology of the Arts implies relative cost increases over time. Some conclude from this that if subsidies are not given, prices would have to rise to such an extent that demand would be reduced almost to zero. The argument fails because many other activities are labour-intensive and do not experience increases in productivity and tend to decline as indeed they should in Pareto optimal situations. If real costs are increasing then such activities should be reduced unless there is an increasing taste for them. In fact there are no features in the Baumol-Bowen model that lead to market failure and they do not themselves seek to justify subsidies in this way.

Some writers, including economists, have thought there might be public good effects or externalities associated with cultural activity which are not reflected in the price of performances. Such things as national or local prestige and a cultured society come under this heading. Two comments are in order. First, no convincing empirical evidence has been offered for the existence of public good effects or externalities. Second, Professor Peacock[2] has pointed out that for these arguments to succeed it must be shown that the cost of acquiring the supposed advantages must be less than the value of benefits and that equal benefits could not be obtained in some other way.

Turning now to increasing returns we ask the question is there anything in the cost structure of the Arts that would cause unit costs to fall as output increases? Performance costs are probably fairly constant and close to marginal costs. But rehearsal costs can be large and do not vary automatically with the number of performances in a fixed ratio. Therefore, as long as programmes are rehearsed average performance cost will be lower the larger the number of performances. Now Pareto optimality requires that prices be set equal to marginal cost so that output is increased only as long as benefits to consumers outweigh the real costs. But if there were excess capacity then this pricing rule would result in a financial deficit; price would be equal to maginal performance cost which would be less than average performance cost including rehearsals. There seems to be a *prima facie* case for subsidies here along lines which have been used extensively by economists to justify subsidies in other fields (e.g. nationalised industries). But more research is needed on the existence and extent of excess capacity and optimal methods of financing the subsidy.

Some economists have considered consumer ignorance to be a possible cause of market failure in the case of the Arts.[3] Ignorance can mean more than one thing. Among the more interesting interpretations are that an ignorant consumer may be uncertain of his preferences or the nature of the product or, he may be mistaken about some characteristics of the product. No doubt both of these interpretations could apply to the Arts. But even if they did, the appropriate form of intervention would be the provision of information rather than more direct support of the Arts. Also, it would have to be demonstrated that the cost of providing information did not exceed the benefits. Since education of this sort is probably labour-intensive and lacking in productivity increases, the real cost of information may be rising over time and would not provide a permanent solution to the problem of the Arts.

Finally, although the Paretian approach has been used extensively in resource allocation problems it is not above criticism. In its usual form it assumes given tastes. If consumer preferences are even slightly dependent on the objects of those preferences, the usual models of social choice and government intervention break down. The evidence of such effects can be found in almost any empirical study of consumer expenditure and it is odd that models of consumer choice have not embodied this feature of the real world.

Although some look to a change in taste as a long run solution to the problems of the Arts[4] it is quite another matter to suggest that public funds should be spent on changing taste. It would be very difficult to argue that this should be done in a way that was not either paternal or dictatorial. However if the 'laws' of taste change were known it might be possible to do so by modifying the Paretian criteria. (We might note in passing that the private sector spends large amounts on changing preferences in favour of 'materialistic' consumption which competes against culture for the consumer's expenditure.)

Notes

1. 'Performing Arts: The Economic Dilemma', MIT Press, 1966.
2. 'Welfare Economics & Public Subsidies To The Arts', Manchester School, 1969.
3. Kling & Blaug, 'Public Patronage of The Arts: The Reasons Why', Encounter, 1973.
4. Peacock, op. cit., p. 322; Skitovsky, 'What's Wrong With The Arts is What's Wrong with Society', American Economic Review, 1972, no. 2.

The Economics of Orchestral Performances

*Roger W. Weiss**

The economies of the orchestra was given its first and still most complete treatment by William Baumol and William Bowen in 1966.[1] Their study is best known for its gloomy predictions of a dynamic gap—of the more rapid rise of cost than demand for orchestral output. They argued that orchestral performance, very labour intensive, would compete with other consumer products, many of which have falling costs from technological advances. Consumers, confronted with this dynamic gap, would allocate a declining part of their budget to live performance, and the orchestra would be faced with the same kind of extinction that has overtaken shoemakers, dressmakers, tailors and cigar-makers.

In the larger American orchestras, concert seasons are organised to provide two or three performances of each programme; thus in Chicago one programme is prepared each week, performed on Thursday and Saturday nights and alternately on Friday or Sunday afternoons or Monday night in a near-by city. In London the four competing orchestras usually perform a programme only once; most of the exceptions are made to allow Royal Festival Hall to be used twice on Sunday, leaving only the morning free for rehearsal. Instead of repeating the afternoon concert and saving a rehearsal, one of the concerts shares some or all of the programme with a concert at an outlying hall earlier in the week.[2] The effect of the allocation of concert dates by the Festival Hall management among the four orchestras is to guarantee a season of a wide selection from the standard repertory and a system that has little scope for efficient reorganisation, depending as it would on the agreement of the orchestras, organised into a cartel (London Orchestral Concert Board), the Arts Council, the Greater London Council and the Musicians Union.

* Professor of Economics, University of Chicago.

Although the data are not perfectly comparable, they indicate a striking contrast between the London and American orchestras in the use of rehearsal and concert time. When we look to data for engagements (performances promoted by others), the ratios are much closer to those of American orchestras. The engaged performances for opera, ballet, tours and school concerts have some repetition of programmes.

Ratios of Rehearsal to Engagement Performances, London Orchestras

	LPO	LSO	NPO	RPO
1972–3	0·7	0·92	0·94	0·84
1971–2	1·03	1·55	0·56	0·92
1970–1	0·88	1·6	1·7	0·88

Source: LOCB *Annual Reports*, Ratios taken of engagement rehearsals to engagements, net of BBC TV, Recording and Film engagements. The engagements include performances at Glyndebourne, in ballet performances, and concerts at festivals, tours and schools.

Ratio of Rehearsals to Concerts,
London and American Orchestras in Self Promoted Concerts

	LPO	LSO	NPO	RPO	BOSTON	CHICAGO	PHILADELPHIA
1972–3	2·56	2·96	2.7	1·94	0·83	0·91	0·93
1971–2	2·04	2·8	3·2	2·3	0·74	0·77	0·97
1970–1	2·4	3·1	3·2	2·3	0·72	1·3	0·91

Source: LOCB, *Annual Reports* and ASOL, Annual *Comparative Reports.*

A London orchestra saves about £600 for each rehearsal eliminated, or about 40 per cent of the present subsidy per concert. Suppose that by repeating programmes the only saving were in rehearsal time (ignoring possible savings in artists' and conductors' fees, and in the printing of programmes and advertising); suppose further the present season of 171 concerts is organised to require 57 programmes, each given three performances. Increase the number of rehearsals for each programme by 0·5, i.e. to 3·0; the total number of rehearsals would fall to 171 from the former level of 428, a saving of 257 rehearsals in the concert season. At roughly £600 per rehearsal, the saving in direct expense would be £154,000 per year, or 75 per cent of the present level of concert subsidies, with benefits in the quality of performances that would increase from the first to the last performance. Touring and the repetition of concerts in near-by cities bring the same benefit, limited by the high cost of transport.

To carry the argument further (stopping short of each orchestra, though not necessarily each conductor, playing only one programme), if each programme were to be given four performances, the forty-three programmes, each given three rehearsals, would save 299 rehearsals, or approximately £180,000 annually, or 90 per cent of the present direct subsidy for London concerts. The 257–300 fewer rehearsals would represent between 53 and 62 per cent of the present work load of one of the orchestras.

Such a radical reorganisation cannot be seriously entertained without careful study. One would need to know much more about the concert going audience before assuming (as this argument has) that the reduction in number of programmes would not also reduce the number of tickets sold either to those who presently go, let us say, more than once a week, or to those whose musical tastes are specialised to a narrow range of composers. A reduction in the number of programmes would reduce the frequency of performance of the repertory by as much as two-thirds. Economists seldom find better examples of the difference between marginal and average cost and the effect of economies of scale. Curiously, it is the monopolistic provincial and American orchestras that have realised these economies, while the oligopolistic and cartelised London orchestras,

Sessions per 1000 Attendance, Selected Orchestras

Year Ending	LONDON ORCHESTRAS 1967	1972	BOSTON 1963	1972	CHICAGO 1964	1972	PHILA- DELPHIA 1963	1972
Total Sessions	667	599	218	360	299	345	296	360
Total Attendance 000s	315	376	286	612	329	477	421	797
Sessions per 1000 Attendance	2·12	1·59	0·76	0·59	0·91	0·72	0·70	0·45
No. Weeks Contract	52	52	50?	52	40[1]	52	37	52

[1] 1964–5

Source: LOCB, *Annual Reports*, ASOL, *Comparative Reports.*

N

organised as producers' co-operatives, have failed to find an efficient organisation of their performances. In private industry there would have been take-over bids and mergers; a notable example in orchestras is the merger of the New York Symphony and the New York Philharmonic Society in 1928.

Although both American and the London orchestras have become more efficient (sessions per 1,000 attendance) in the past decade, it is only the London orchestras, whose concerts are their minor activity, for which reorganisation could bring a dramatic reduction in deficit. Their dependency on engagement and recording sessions for the major part of their incomes has kept them in the traditional position of selling their services, collectively, as freelance musicians, at the session rates. The central staffs and office overheads needed for organising their collective activity are quite small. All of the work undertaken by the orchestras is therefore priced at the marginal cost of providing it. The provincial orchestras in Britain and America all have been organised by voluntary associations of patrons in areas where local demand was not sufficient to hold the musicians in the community. With costs contracted over a whole season, these orchestras more easily could disregard the marginal cost pricing of their services.

The initial premise of Baumol and Bowen that technology has passed over the performing arts was not strictly accurate; the long-playing record and tape recordings, radio and television have brought a revolution in the cost of reaching audiences. British concerts are broadcast to radio audiences of 100,000 and television audiences between 1,000,000 and 6,000,000. A long-playing record costing one pound, played, let us say, ten times, brings music to the listener's home at a cost of 10p per performance. The same performance can be provided at a cost of 3p and 0·3p per listener to radio and television respectively, assuming audiences of the size estimated above and costs that include the full promoted concert costs less ticket revenues from the attending audiences. There may be advantages and disadvantages from listening to recorded and broadcast music; broadcast music loses some of the fidelity, balance and excitement of the concert hall, depending partly on the quality of the receiving equipment. But there are some gains in comfort and savings in time and expense of travel to and from the concert. A recorded performance is usually more accurate but sometimes less inspired than live performances. But technology has greatly reduced the cost of hearing music and it allows reaching an audience that cannot come to the concert hall by reason of being tied to the house by small children, sickness, age, poverty and distance, and it permits a variety of choice over repertory, performers and the time of performance not available to concert-goers, regardless of their means and location. A cheapening of cost in the order of magnitude of 90 per cent matches the most important consumer products. Baumol and Bowen, in concentrating on live performances, were not encouraged by this prospect.[3]

Under the impact of such a cheapening of cost, other things being equal, we might expect a concentration of output into the hands of the most efficient firms, a decline in the number of orchestras, perhaps, and a decline in live performance in favour of recorded and broadcast performances. The average quality of performance might rise considerably, and the orchestras that survived would combine concert activity with broadcast and recording. The recording industry would, as it has, migrate to countries with the lowest wage costs, and the high wage countries would suffer from the competition of expensive live concerts with cheap recordings; the resistance of demand for live performance to increased prices might be greatest in the high wage countries.

The cheapened cost of recorded music against the escalating cost of live concerts would surely have had devastating consequences in an ordinary market; that the number of concerts has risen in the past fifteen years argues for a large shift in demand in favour of concerts. But the orchestras have been able to take little advantage of the opportunities of sharing rehearsal costs among live, recorded and broadcast performances. In Britain the BBC organised its own orchestra in the late Twenties when no alternative existed in London. But instead of using its patronage to strengthen the provincial orchestras, it created parallel and independent establishments in Manchester and Glasgow.[4]

The London orchestras derive between 20 and 33 per cent of their employment from making recordings. With session costs almost four times as high as those of London orchestras, few American orchestras derive a net revenue from recordings; a few orchestras seem to subsidise their recordings.

Touring and the repetition of concerts in near-by cities have traditionally provided the means for 'extending production runs'; the Hallé Orchestra regularly took its programme to Liverpool; the Scottish National Orchestra repeats its concerts in Glasgow and Edinburgh; the Chicago Symphony Orchestra plays in Milwaukee, Wisconsin. High transportation costs, the high value of musicians' leisure time and the element of local pride all stand in the way of extending the market, but there may be an unrealised potential in reorganising seasons in Boston, New York, Philadelphia and Washington for regular exchanges of programme; possibly Chicago, Cleveland, Detroit and Milwaukee could similarly federate.

Where summers were hot and patrons left the city, concerts were organised in the open air; British and American orchestras still have summer seasons in suburbs or resort areas. With poor acoustics, the interference of airplanes, trains and insects, these settings provide a poor environment for refined performances of a major orchestra. Perhaps air conditioning of the concert hall can provide a superior alternative.

Although on the Continent most symphonic music is provided by opera orchestras, there are few cases in Britain or the United States of sharing an orchestra for both functions. The LPO plays for the summer Glyndebourne season and the San Francisco Symphony plays a regular opera season. Although few operas call for as large an orchestra as late nineteenth-century symphonies, there are potential savings in the sharing of orchestras, apparently not presently being realised when 20–40 members are paid not to play.

Another means of economising might call for splitting the large orchestra of 100–110 instruments into two smaller ensembles, each of a size appropriate to much contemporary music and to the repertory composed before about 1850. There could be economies from concert series in outlying areas with smaller halls. The Peacock committee heard strong evidence against dividing orchestras, where the experience of one orchestra was a decline in the quality of the ensemble of the divided orchestra and of the reunited orchestra. Yet on the face of it, the variety afforded by the chamber orchestra repertory, the stimulus to the musician from being able to hear and play with others to whom he cannot relate in the full orchestra might be very valuable to the members. Recently Pierre Boulez recommended that 'the orchestra of the future' be formed from various small groupings 'split up into quartets, chamber groups and contemporary ensembles, so that ... they could hear themselves play for a change.'[5] The smaller groupings that enable the orchestra member to grow in his musicianship also might afford reaching new audiences in new locations with a better potential for covering the cost of performing than either the full orchestra in the new location or in an additional concert in their usual hall.

If orchestral performance were left to a private market to organise, undoubtedly many changes would be made from the present patterns of seasonal concerts and repertory. Ticket prices in America would rise by a third to as much as double their present levels and the quantity and perhaps the quality of performance would fall back. In America and the British provincial cities, performance has, from very early on, been organised by voluntary associations of patrons whose contributions made possible the establishment of larger orchestras performing longer seasons and perhaps different repertory than the alternatives of proprietary orchestras or players' co-operatives would have provided. Over considerable periods little subsidy was needed to maintain the orchestras. When contributions were needed to fill the 'dynamic gap', they could be rationalised in economic vocabulary as a means of tapping the consumers' surplus orchestral performance created.

In the United States, where personal and corporate taxes permit the deduction of philanthropic contributions before applying the tax rate to net income, a community has an incentive to price tickets below the market clearing levels. Assuming there are no difficulties in a community forming a voluntary association that can assess itself without problems from 'free riders' and all members are, e.g. in a 50 per cent marginal tax bracket, the optimal allocation of contributions to ticket purchases would be in the ratio of two to one, far higher than any orchestra in practice has arranged overall, although not perhaps for those patrons in certain tax brackets.

*Contributions to American Orchestras
from the Private Sector, 1971–2*

	BOSTON	CLEVE-LAND	PHILA-DELPHIA	CHICAGO	NEW YORK	LOS ANGELES
As Per Cent of Ticket Sales	51	75·5	32·5	101·0	46·5	51·3
As Per Cent of Expenditures	41·3	49·2	20·2	50·6	36·6	30·4

Source: ASOL, *Major Symphony Orchestras, Comparative Report.*

The orchestral patron thus has two motives to contribute to his orchestra: as a means by which a voluntary association can appropriate enough from consumers' surplus to justify a natural monopoly, and in a manner to take advantage of savings in income taxes in doing so. Beyond these, 'pure' motives of philanthropy may explain the support for orchestras. Typically orchestras in America are organised as consumers' voluntary associations with decisions about the quality and scale of output vested in representatives of consumers or that portion of consumers who are major contributors.

In Britain orchestral performance is subsidised by municipal and state authorities. In the provinces the pattern of consumers' voluntary association dominates; in London the orchestras are producers' co-operatives. Between 33 and 43 per cent of the total income of the London orchestras from public concerts is provided by the London Orchestral Concert Board.

Direct Subsidy as a Percentage of Total Revenue
(*Self Promoted Concerts*)

	LPO	LSO	NPO	RPO	REGIONAL ORCHESTRAS
1971–2	32	33	39	33	
1970–1	36	38	32	42	
1969–70	35	34	37	43	
1968–9					52

Source: L O C B, *Annual Report* and *Peacock Report*, Table 2.

Under the present organisation of subsidies in Britain, the Arts Council determines the number of orchestras to which it will commit public subsidy and provides the level of support necessary to insure the continuing life of the orchestra. 'It is a matter of some pride in the whole of the Council's history, with supported organizations now exceeding 1,000, there have only been two or three examples of an enterprise which, for purely financial reasons, had to be wound up,'[6] is their way of stating it. Whether such a record is enviable cannot be decided on the face of this statement; it is often difficult and arbitrary to determine a single cause of death. But changing circumstances ought to call for the consolidation or termination of some activities in the arts as well as starting new ones, and a certain mortality rate might be a healthy adjustment of resources in the arts as it is in market-oriented activities. The location, quality and quantity of output are decided in production for markets by an interaction of demand and supply for which financial deficits and surpluses are valuable indicators and rather stern disciplinarians. Ought there to be something equivalent in the supply of the arts?

Subsidy as a Percentage of Total Revenue
of British Regional Orchestras, 1968–9

BOURNEMOUTH	BIRMINGHAM	HALLÉ	LIVERPOOL	SCOTTISH NATIONAL
53·5	56·1	44·0	58·0	64·5

Source: *Peacock Report*, Table 1.

At present, when the concert-goer spends £1·00 on a ticket, the social resources he calls to be expended are £1·50 in London, £2·38 in Liverpool and £2·82 in Glasgow. If we value the patrons equally, we might take their willingness to spend £1·00 on a concert as equivalent in value. We might conclude that resources ought best to be allocated to uses where equal amounts yield equal value to consumers. By this guideline the Arts Council might move to reduce concert activity, raise ticket prices or search for cost savings in areas where the return to public expenditure seems lower than in other areas. There are many extenuating considerations, no doubt, before this simple financial guideline should be allowed to rule.

The orchestra is a firm hiring very specialised resources capable of playing a variety of musical compositions. From training and experience, its performers have become habituated to the styles of performance best suited to music of the period between Beethoven and Mahler, but they also perform the styles from Handel to Mozart and from Debussy to many of the present day. Not all of these styles are equally congenial to the typical orchestra and many do not require the full complement of instruments, usually from 90 to 110. In the better orchestras the players develop a fine articulation and sensitivity to one another, and under the best conditions, play with a precision, balance and tonal beauty that even very skilled players, brought together occasionally, cannot match. These qualities often are the individual mark of a great conductor, a Stokowski, or Karajan.

The specialised orchestral organisation is usually a monopolist in its local market and usually performs a range of types of programme: popular, symphonic, summer etc. It goes on tour to avoid saturating its local market, plays for a season of opera and perhaps of ballet from the same motives as an automobile manufacturer who extends his range of cars to be assembled on the same lines.

Henry Wood's Proms were held nightly with only one rehearsal. Monteverdi's *Arianna* was rehearsed for five months. Rodzinski was accustomed to rehearse an orchestra in three hours before making a recording of a symphony. There is no *a priori* standard of performance required in any composer's specifications. A range of preparation is determined by the interaction of supply and demand in the market.

The best choice of the appropriate mixture of repertories, of standards in rehearsal, of the schedule of an orchestra's concerts, whether at home, on tour, in divided groups or in seasons of opera, oratorio and pops, is the function of the entrepreneur-impresario, acting on his insight into his market and on the constraints of costs, and learning from his successes and failures and those of others.

Diversity and a multitude of independent experiments at home and abroad in higher as well as lower quality help to establish appropriate adjustments to changing tastes and economic conditions.

The new role of the state in patronage of the arts in Britain and the United States shifts the locus of decision making. The level of state subsidy becomes the independent determinant of the quantity (and quality) of output. At the same time, with output brought to a level where little performance can be undertaken by private promotion, the entry of new organisations depends on access to subsidy. The state patron of the arts must exercise discretion in choosing from the multitude of applications those that will be supported. With the best of intentions, it cannot avoid this discretion as long as its subsidy has already brought the level of output beyond the break-even point.

It is likely that the state will be conservative in its patronage and that its agency will support the established institutions around which strong vested interests develop. It may at the same time parcel out small sums to a multitude of other groups that clamour for support. In the experience of the London orchestras, the role of the state has been to support a large increase in performance but with a remarkably inefficient organisation. The effect of a centralised and bureaucratic agency of public subsidy may be to weaken the decision-making functions.

The work of the economist is to examine alternatives and point out their costs. Whenever public resources are used for one among the multiplicity of competing activities of government, it is appropriate that the costs and criteria of efficient utilisation are made explicit. Those whose task it is to examine these costs will always seem to be asking for retrenchment and a cheapening of standards and may in truth lack the courage and imagination to justify new ventures. But their readers will be those with strong interests favouring subsidy.

The foregoing discussion has concentrated on looking at the output of music 'at its margins', at the cost and revenue from an additional concert and at potential savings in creating joint products. Other economic questions important to the performing arts are the analysis of demand for concerts and the analysis of the criteria for directing subsidy. The economist's role, notwithstanding the current swell in his interest in the arts, must remain subordinate; the world will still need a Boyd Neel to bring forward a new interpretation of Handel, a Theodore Thomas to develop public acceptance of the symphonic repertory, a Henry Wood to exploit the demand for cheap concerts, and, perhaps, a Toscanini to excite listeners. The conductor may always hold the key to the survival of performing.

Let us hope that the mysterious entrepreneurial art survives the new role of centralised patronage in our age of bureaucrats and economists.

Notes

1. William Baumol and William Bowen, *The Performing Arts—The Economic Dilemma*, New York, The Twentieth Century Fund, 1966. The following abbreviations will be used throughout this article: LCCB, London Orchestral Concert Board, Ltd: ASOL, American Symphony Orchestra League, Vienna, Virginia; LPO, London Philharmonic Orchestra; LSO, London Symphony Orchestra; NPO, New Philharmonia Orchestra; RPO, Royal Philharmonic Orchestra; *Peacock Report*, Arts Council of Great Britain, *A Report on Orchestral Resources in Great Britain, 1970*.
2. The lesson of the distinguished Courtauld-Sargent concerts organised each season between 1929 and 1939 was forgotten. Among the principles of the series, there was to be no deputising, each concert was to be rehearsed three times and repeated at least once (in the 1932–3 season, twice).
3. Baumol and Bowen see technological change mainly as a threat to the (live) performing arts. 'Progress in general technology has had a considerable impact on the arts through new methods of presentation of performances to the public. The development of motion pictures, phonograph records, radio and television has caused a precipitous drop in the cost of providing an hour of entertainment to each member of the audience. But these innovations have not helped the live performing arts directly; in fact, the competition of the mass media for both audience and artistic personnel has sometimes had serious consequences for performing organizations,' (p. 390).
4. For data on performers and orchestras, see BBC, *BBC Handbook 1974*, London, 1973, pp. 260–2, and the Peacock Report, pp. 47–54.
5. Peacock Report, quoting the Scottish Arts Council, 'Frequent division of an orchestra is as bad for the whole as it is for the parts,' (p. 25), to which they add the statement of Thurston Dart, 'Any of us who have worked for decades with chamber orchestras know that it is *not* possible to carve a chamber orchestra out of a small symphony orchestra (of say 65 players) or a large symphony orchestra (of say 105 players). The styles of playing are different, as are the assignments of responsibility.' But Pierre Boulez argues that musicians need the variety of styles and changes in ensemble in order to fulfil their potential. See the paraphrase of his remarks to the New York Chapter of the American Musicological Society published in *Musical Newsletter*, IV, I, Winter 1974, p. 21.
6. Sir Hugh Willatt. *The Arts Council of Great Britain, The First Twenty-Five Years*, London. s.d. p. 10.

Index